BOOK BUDDIES

Guidelines for Volunteer Tutors of Emergent and Early Readers

Francine R. Johnston, EdD
University of North Carolina at Greensboro, NC

Marcia Invernizzi, PhD
University of Virginia, Charlottesville, VA

Connie Juel, PhD
University of Virginia, Charlottesville, VA

The Guilford Press
New York   London

© 1998 The Guilford Press
A Division of Guilford Publications, Inc.
72 Spring Street, New York, NY 10012
http://www.guilford.com

Printed in the United States of America

This book is printed in acid-free paper.

Last digit is print number: 9 8 7 6 5 4 3 2

Library of Congress-Cataloging-in-Publication Data

Johnston, Francine R.
    Book buddies : guidelines for volunteer tutors of emergent and
early readers / Francine R. Johnston, Marcia Invernizzi, Connie Juel.
        p. cm.
    Includes bibliographical references and index.
    ISBN 1-57230-347-6 (paperback)
    1. Volunteer workers in education—United States. 2. Reading
teachers—United States. 3. Reading—United States. 4. Tutors and
tutoring—United States. I. Invernizzi, Marcia. II. Juel, Connie.
III. Title.
LB2844.1.V6J65 1998
371.14'124—dc21   98-2639
                                                                    CIP

Preface

Stanley walks into Greenhill Elementary School. His mind shifts gears from concern over his own work to how the child he tutors, Malcolm, always beams when he sees Stanley enter his classroom. Sure enough, there's that smile, thinks Stanley as he goes into the corner of the classroom to sit at a small table with Malcolm. Malcolm tells Stanley he's going to be fast today because he's been practicing his words.

Stanley takes four books out of the box of materials he brought for the tutoring session. Malcolm, however, has other plans. He is eager to begin the tutoring session by reading from a collection of words, called a word bank. Stanley says to hold on, they'll get there, but first they will start as they always do by rereading some books. Stanley chides Malcolm, "You can practice being fast reading these books. Which book do you want to start reading?"

Malcolm selects the book *Sandy*. He says that Sandy always gets scared about that dog. "Right," agrees Stanley. "And, what was it about that dog that scared him?" Malcolm says the dog was real mean and then he picks up the book. Malcolm reads, "A man ran. . . . " As he reaches the word "past," he stops and looks at Stanley. Stanley points to the letter "p" in the printed word and suggests Malcolm use the first sound. Malcolm says the sound of "p," which is just enough information to help him identify "past" in the story he has read before.

Stanley is very proud of the work he does with Malcolm. Malcolm seems to benefit because his reading is improving, and because he delights in the fact that an adult cares enough about him to come and see him twice a week. As Malcolm was heard saying to a friend, "He comes just to see me!" It is indeed the combined bond of caring *and* the one-on-one work on reading that seem to make tutoring so effective (Invernizzi, Rosemary, Juel, & Richards, 1997; Juel, 1991, 1996).

The individualized help that Stanley provides Malcolm—feedback and assistance that is perfectly geared to Malcolm's current understandings about how print works—is much easier to provide in one-on-one tutoring than it is in a bustling classroom of young children. When Malcolm's knowledge of letters, sounds, and words is more advanced, Stanley will adjust his form of interac-

Figure 1 Malcom and Stanley

tion. He will expect more from Malcolm and challenge him to use his new knowledge to identify unknown words. In the future, for example, Stanley might see if Malcolm can identify "past" by using knowledge of the consonants "s" and "t" in addition to the initial "p," or, when Malcolm knows the short "a," pointing to the "a." Individualized feedback at just the right time in just the right books is what makes successful tutoring.

Once, you were like Malcolm. Once, nearly every word was a struggle. Now it is your turn to help someone learn to read. This book has been written as a guide for both program coordinators of volunteer staffed reading tutorials as well as for the tutors themselves. Chapter 1 explains why we believe the tutorial we present in this guidebook is an effective model for the use of volunteers. Chapter 2 provides information and tips for the coordinators who are responsible for organizing a program, for writing lesson plans, and for training and supervising tutors. Chapter 3 contains the assessment tools and information needed for determining individual children's needs. Chapters 4 and 5 describe in detail exactly what tutors need to do to work effectively with their children. The Appendices contain many helpful forms and supplementary information needed to implement a volunteer tutoring program. To learn how to obtain copies of the guidebook at special quantity discounts, and for details on our two companion training videos, see page 165.

We wish you the best in your efforts. Volunteers *can* make a tremendous difference in the lives and the literacy skills of our children.

Acknowledgments

Development of the volunteer reading tutorial known as Book Buddies has been supported by grants from the Hershey Foundation of Cleveland, Ohio, the Inez D. Bishop Foundation of Charlottesville, Virginia, and the Charlottesville Albemarle Foundation for Excellence. Without the support provided by these grants, the development activity required for this volunteer tutorial would not have been possible.

Book Buddies is an adaptation and expansion of Darrell Morris's Howard Street Tutoring Project (Morris, Shaw, & Perney, 1990). We are indebted to Darrell for his inspiration and lead. We are also indebted to several cohorts of graduate students from the University of Virginia McGuffey Reading Center, many of whom have been and still are Book Buddies site coordinators. We particularly wish to thank Mary Boylin and Laura McMahon, who have contributed directly to this tutoring manual, and to Cathy Rosemary for her help with the research.

Thanks are also extended to Arletta Dimburg, Assistant Superintendent of the Charlottesville City Schools, as well as Malcolm Jarrell and Nancy Toms, former and current Intervention Coordinators for the Charlottesville Schools. Special thanks goes to the many volunteers who have given their time and talents to the children of Charlottesville, and to Mary Ann Elwood and Eleanor Kett, who recruited them.

References

Invernizzi, M., Rosemary, C., Juel, C., & Richards, H. (1997). At-risk readers and community volunteers: A three year perspective. *Scientific Studies of Reading, 1*(3), 277–300.

Juel, C. (1991). Cross-age tutoring between student athletes and at-risk children. *The Reading Teacher, 45,* 178–186.

Juel, C. (1996). What makes literacy tutoring effective? *Reading Research Quarterly, 31,* 268–289.

Morris, O., Shaw, B., & Perney, J. (1990). Helping low readers in grades 2 and 3: An after-school volunteer tutoring program. *The Elementary School Journal, 91, 2,* 133–150.

Contents

Evaluating Beginning Readers 31

General Tutoring Plan for the Emergent Reader 61

General Tutoring Plan for the Early Reader 101

CHAPTER 1

Volunteer Tutorials

The America Reads Challenge

A fundamental component of the America Reads Challenge is the creation of America's Reading Corps to ensure that all children are able to read independently and well by the end of third grade (U.S. Department of Education [USDOE], 1997a). Toward that end, the President of the United States has called for a national, bipartisan effort to recruit and place as many as one million volunteer reading tutors in elementary schools across the country.

The President's proposal is an ambitious one, and one that has gained the attention of educators, researchers, policymakers, and community members across the country. An enormous amount of money has been proposed to fund this initiative. An enormous amount of labor is being solicited as well. As many as 11,000 members of AmeriCorps, the federal program that offers young adults college tuition aid in return for community service, plan to mobilize volunteers in the next few years (Manzo & Sack, 1997). Education Secretary Richard Riley has stated that he will work with religious leaders across the country to rally tens of thousands of volunteers (Riley, 1997). Already, there is financial support available for 100,000 college work–study students to serve as reading tutors. Sixty presidents of postsecondary institutions have pledged their support by designating nearly 10,000 work–study positions for reading tutors (USDOE, 1997b).

Such massive recruiting efforts inevitably lead to the critical question concerning the role that these volunteers will play in the literacy development of children who need help. Specifically, what will volunteers be asked to do, and how will they be trained and supported in their efforts? These essential questions have not yet been systematically answered. Although 330,000 reading specialists and tutor coordinators are being summoned to mobilize and train this corps of volunteers, the format and type of training is not delineated (USDOE, 1997b).

Across the nation, well-intentioned schools and communities are scrambling to locate successful tutoring programs—programs that can be replicated, modified, or used in some way—as they plan their responses to America Reads (Manzo & Sack, 1997). Although hundreds of grassroots volunteer tutoring efforts already exist (several of which are cited in America Reads documents), we actually know very little about their effectiveness (Wasik, 1997; Manzo & Sack, 1997). Given the current political climate and the spotlight on volunteer tutoring efforts, the need for extensive evaluation of existing programs and for the replication of successful ones is especially pressing. School divisions nationwide need alternative, affordable models of effective early literacy intervention programs so that they can make informed decisions as they attempt to best meet the needs of their students with the limited resources they have available. As Wasik (1997) aptly concludes, it seems that the real challenge of America Reads is to implement effective, well-evaluated, and readily replicable programs in schools, to increase the level of literacy learning of our nation's children (p. 33).

Well-researched, professionally organized intervention programs such as Reading Recovery (Clay, 1985) and Success for All (Slavin, Madden, Karwait, Dolan, & Wasik, 1993) have demonstrated substantial positive effects for students individually tutored by a trained professional. Few would argue that using specifically trained professionals in early literacy interventions is preferable to having a volunteer attempt to fill this role. However, this is not always possible. The extensive training required of most tutor/teachers, as well as the limited number of students each teacher is able to tutor, make one-on-one programs that use highly trained teachers as tutors too expensive for many school districts, especially those with many needy children (Invernizzi, Rosemary, Juel, & Richards, 1997).

Given the growing number of children who need additional literacy support and the reality of budget constraints, many schools districts have been forced to consider less expensive means of providing early intervention (Invernizzi, et al., 1997; Wasik, 1997). One source of additional help historically has been volunteer efforts within local communities.

Unfortunately, many well-intentioned programs using volunteers as tutors do not have data to empirically support their efforts; thus, little information can be gleaned regarding their effect on children's reading abilities (Wasik, 1997). Existing volunteer tutoring programs seem to run the gamut in terms of the method and amount of training that volunteers are given, the degree of tutor supervision, and the materials and methods used in instruction. They also vary greatly in how their students are assessed and how their programs are evaluated. In fact, many local programs presently contain no measure of evaluating student's reading growth (Wasik, 1997).

Empirically Researched Volunteer Tutoring Programs

Promising work using volunteers as tutors has been documented in the research. Darrell Morris used volunteer tutors, trained and supervised by graduate students, in an after-school tutoring program outside of Chicago. The volunteer tutors of the Howard Street Program delivered a balanced instructional plan that included multiple rereading of familiar text, word study, and guided reading. Morris, Shaw, and Perney (1990) reported significant gains in reading graded basal passages (from 0.5 to 1.5 grade levels) for the tutored group compared to matched controls. These gains suggest that nonprofessional volunteers can deliver effective intervention if trained and supported by certified teachers knowledgeable of how children learn to read.

Juel's cross-age tutoring program using university student athletes, who were themselves poor readers, also yielded positive results. The mean score of the tutored children on the reading comprehension subtest of the Iowa Tests of Basic Skills was at the 41st percentile, compared to a mean score at the 16th percentile for nontutored controls (Juel, 1991, 1996). Tutors improved their own reading while they tutored.

Charlottesville's volunteer tutorial, known locally as Book Buddies, has also reaped notable results. Book Buddies uses community volunteers who teach from a lesson plan prepared by reading specialists. The volunteers are trained and supported on-site throughout the year. Analyses of the program over the years has revealed the growing efficacy of the program. Children with greater than 40 sessions have significantly outperformed children with fewer than 40 tutoring sessions on most pre- and posttest gain scores, and on both outcome measures of text reading and word recognition. Effect sizes for gains in word recognition have been considerably higher than effect sizes reported for other tutorials using paraprofessionals and volunteers—has as high as +1.29 (Invernizzi et al., 1997). These gains are particularly impressive when one considers the cost-effectiveness of the program: The average cost per child is around $600, approximately one-sixth the cost of professional, trademarked tutorials using highly trained intervention specialists (see Hiebert, 1994). The gains over the years have demonstrated that two sessions of one-on-one tutoring per week, by a trained, supported, and supervised community volunteer for a minimum of 20 weeks, can be an effective and affordable alternative intervention for children at risk for reading failure. In her review of existing volunteer tutorials, Wasik (1997) acknowledged Book Buddies as a well-designed, systematic program developed by researchers who are experts in the field (p. 12).

The key to these successful volunteer efforts is most likely to be the training and close supervision given to the tutors. In the Howard Street and Book Buddies programs, for example, the lesson plans were prepared by knowledgeable reading educators, and the volunteer tutors were guided on-site, lesson-by-lesson, throughout the year. Juel's tutors, who were working on their own reading and writing skills, were students in her reading course.

The Charlottesville Book Buddies Program

Book Buddies is the first large-scale model to mobilize hundreds of community volunteers in an alternative one-on-one intervention. Book Buddies was developed as a joint effort between the Charlottesville City Schools, the University of Virginia, and the community of Charlottesville (see Invernizzi, Juel, & Rosemary, 1996). It was adopted as part of the school division's long-range plan that all children read independently by third grade. Beginning as a grant-supported program, Book Buddies is now a totally self-sustaining volunteer tutorial, fully funded by the Charlottesville City Schools.

To date, the program has served over 700 children in grades one and two. The tutoring guide has been used by over 300 volunteers for the past 6 years and has been revised and expanded based on our experience and research

Book Buddies received the 1997 Literacy Award from the Virginia State Reading Association and has been replicated and adapted throughout the State of Virginia and in several states across the nation (Caserta-Henry, 1996). The program is currently being replicated in Cleveland, Ohio, and in the South Bronx by the Experience Corp. (an intergenerational project of the Community Service Society of New York), a project supported by the National Corporation for Service and Vista Volunteers as part of the America Reads Challenge.

Program Description

Book Buddies has several unique features. To recruit volunteer tutors, a volunteer recruiter solicits interested community members through the media, public meetings with community service groups, business associations, and personal contacts. Each tutor is trained in research-based methods two to three times per year during whole-group, 2-hour training sessions. Each session incorporates video demonstration lessons of actual tutorials and a walk-through of the lesson plan.

At each school, a site coordinator provides ongoing training and support for the tutors by writing daily lesson plans, arranging materials for each lesson, and providing routine feedback regarding specific activities and techniques. Each site coordinator supervises 15 volunteer tutors and their respective tutees at the 45-minute, biweekly sessions.

Settings for the tutorials vary depending on individual classroom teacher preferences and school resources. The majority of the tutorials are in-school pull-outs occurring in separate classrooms designated as tutoring centers. Tutorials should be scheduled to avoid conflicts with academic instruction in the classroom. Recently, Book Buddies has expanded to include an after-school model delivered by federally funded work–study students as part of the America Reads Challenge.

Coordinators, Tutors, and Children

The heart of the Book Buddies tutorial is a triad composed of the site coordinator, the volunteer tutor, and the child. The site coordinators, each of whom is a reading specialist, supervise the volunteers and provide ongoing support throughout the duration of the program. Their responsibilities include (1) assessing students individually three times a year to design an appropriate instructional program and to monitor children's progress; (2) training and providing continual support for volunteers; (3) coordinating the instructional program with the classroom teacher and Title I teacher; (4) writing individualized lesson plans to assure that the needs of each student are being met; and (5) documenting time, testing data, and anecdotal information regarding the program. Site coordinators report the children's progress to parents and teachers through conferences and written correspondence. They are paid by the public schools and work approximately 15–17 hours per week to support and supervise their volunteers and students.

The volunteer recruiter matches the schedules and number of volunteers needed at each elementary school with the schedules of volunteers who are available during particular times. The reading coordinators meet regularly with each other and are in constant communication with the volunteer recruiter and central office personnel. Children who move to another school are not lost in the shuffle, but are instead picked up by the coordinator at that school and assigned a tutor. Occasionally, tutors even move to a new school with the child.

The tutors are primarily volunteers from the Charlottesville community. About one-fourth of them leave their job to tutor during work hours. The volunteers come from all walks of life, from rug cleaners and rock-and-roll musicians, to retired senior citizens, realtors, and city councilors. Females outnumber male volunteers by four to one. The ages of the tutors are evenly split across the age brackets of 20–39, 40–59, and 60 years and above. The staying power of our volunteers is remarkable: 96% of the volunteer tutors complete the full school year, 63% have tutored for 2 years, and 45% have tutored 3 years or more. The volunteers are educated, middle-class citizens who want to change the world.

The volunteer tutors have several responsibilities. They attend whole-group training sessions two times per year. They arrive for the tutorial ahead of time to review the lesson plan for the day and to ask questions if necessary. They follow the instructional plan developed for their child by the site coordinator, and they provide written evaluation following each tutorial. After the tutorial, volunteer tutors meet informally with their site coordinator to give and receive feedback on their lesson. Communication is maintained on a regular basis through personal contacts, telephone conversations, and written exchanges.

The children are primarily first-grade students recommended for the program by their classroom teachers. Student selection is collaboratively determined, taking into account the school's own assessment, teacher observations, the children's scores on the Book Buddies assessment (see Chapter 3), and the school's own resources to service their children in need of additional instruction. First-grade children are served first, but some second graders are included as well. Second graders are tutored depending on the availability of resources and sometimes because the volunteer tutors want to work with their child for another year. On the average, 55% of the children are male, and 45% are female; 63% are African American, 35% are Caucasian, and 2% are from other ethnic groups. Seventy percent of the children qualify for free lunch.

The Tutoring Lesson

The tutoring lesson consists of reading, writing, and phonics. Tutors follow a sequence of core activities planned by the site coordinators in a four-part lesson plan described in Chapters 4 and 5. The balanced plan includes practice reading for fluency and comprehension, direct instruction in the systematic correspondences between sounds, letters and spelling patterns, and writing, and contains many of the components of effective tutoring identified by Juel's (1996) research.

Book Buddies is based on several assumptions gleaned from previous research on effective tutoring:

1. Children learn to read by reading in meaningful contexts.

2. Reading instruction should be differentiated based on diagnosed learner needs.

3. Phonics instruction should be taught systematically and paced according to a child's developing hypotheses about how words work.

4. Reading, writing, and spelling develop in synchrony.

5. Learning to read occurs in a social context and through interactions with a more knowledgeable other.

Children are provided with multiple opportunities to reread text, and the tutors enable them to complete tasks they wouldn't otherwise be able to do by modeling and scaffolding. With the ongoing assistance of the site coordinator, volunteers provide appropriate-level instruction and written materials at the right time (Juel, 1996).

Program Results over Time

Our research over the years has demonstrated that quality instruction can be delivered by community volunteers if they are properly supported. Book Buddies has continued to get stronger over time, as shown in posttest outcome measures that have improved steadily across the years. Each successive year has produced significantly more children who can read *Little Bear* (Minarik, 1957) with 90% accuracy. (*Little Bear* is a benchmark book selected by first-grade teachers as a hallmark of successful reading). For the past 3 years, 86–89% of *all* first-grade Book Buddies students could read *Little Bear* with greater than 90% accuracy by the end of the year. This percentage increases for children who receive more than 40 tutoring sessions. As a check on criterion indicators of growth, raw scores for the word reading subtest on the Wide Range Achievement Test (WRAT; Jastak & Wilkinson, 1984) have also been compared by program year, and these have also improved steadily over time. In the fifth year of the program, 88% of all first-grade Book Buddies children scored at the mid- to end-first-grade level on the WRAT, a standardized, norm-referenced test of word recognition.

The Hidden Benefits of Volunteer Tutoring

Educational researchers and policymakers have called for greater community involvement in schools and for schools to reach out to communities for supportive services. Volunteer tutorials combine the concern, expertise, and human resources inherent in every community, its schools, and its universities. Volunteer tutorials offer one model of an affordable, alternative form of early intervention that can help meet the needs of a struggling community. And according to one of our volunteers, Millie, "There's a lot of love that comes from it actually."

Book Buddies, the volunteer tutorial from which this manual evolved, has generated many other immeasurable benefits. Volunteer tutors have gained an appreciation for the diversity of the student population and the challenges such diversity presents to the classroom teacher. They have begun to understand the political rhetoric behind the publicized debate between phonics versus whole language and have acquired a deeper sense of the complexity of learning how to read. Site coordinators, specialists in reading education, have learned to translate pedagogy into common sense and have become skilled in the art of communication and persuasion. University faculty have learned what it takes to become trusted by a school division. Teachers and other school personnel have learned to reach out to the community for help to accomplish what they cannot do alone. And the children have learned to read.

Setting Up a Volunteer Tutorial

In setting up a volunteer reading tutorial, it is important to collaborate with school personnel and community leaders. We advise starting small, perhaps at one school. Evaluate the effectiveness of your program, fine-tune, and expand as personnel and materials become available.

Volunteer tutorials can take place before, during, or after school. In some schools, reading specialists and classroom teachers have worked together as reading coordinators. In this situation, teaching loads have been adjusted to provide time for coordinating duties. In other instances, teachers who have been trained in early intervention methods earn additional stipends for staying after school to supervise community volunteers who come in to tutor. The classroom teachers write the lesson plans and guide the volunteers as they work one-on-one with their children.

Whatever model you adopt, the role of on-site volunteer coordinators is vital. Their role as team leaders will be described in the next chapter.

References

Caserta-Henry, C. (1996). Reading buddies: A first grade reading intervention program. *The Reading Teacher, 49,* 500–503.

Clay, M. M. (1985). *The early detection of reading difficulties.* Portsmouth, NH: Heinemann.

Hiebert, E. H. (1994). Reading recovery in the United States: What difference does it make to an age cohort? *Educational Researcher, 23,* 15–25.

Invernizzi, M., Rosemary, C., Juel, C., & Richards, H. (1997). At-risk readers and community volunteers: A three year perspective. *Scientific Studies of Reading, 1*(3), 277–300.

Invernizzi, M., Juel, C., & Rosemary, C. A. (1996). A community volunteer tutorial that works. *The Reading Teacher, 50,* 304–311.

Jastak, S., & Wilkinson, G. S. (1984). *Wide range achievement test—Revised.* Wilmington, DE: Jastak Associates.

Juel, C. (1996). What makes literacy tutoring effective? *Reading Research Quarterly, 31,* 268–289.

Juel, C. (1991). Cross-age tutoring between student athletes and at-risk children. *The Reading Teacher, 45,* 178–186.

Manzo, K. K., & Sack, J. L. (1997, February 26). Effectiveness of Clinton reading plan questioned. *Education Week.* [On-line]. http://www.edweek.org.

Minarik, E. H. (1957). *Little Bear.* New York: Harper Trophy.

Morris, D., Shaw, B., & Perney, J. (1990). Helping low readers in grades 2 and 3: An after-school volunteer tutoring program. *Elementary School Journal, 91,* 133–150.

Riley, R. W. (1997). Press briefing on the President's 1998 budget. [On-line]. http://www.ed.gov.

Slavin, R., Madden, N., Karweit, N., Dolan, L., & Wasik, B. (1993). Success for all: Longitudinal effects of a restructuring program for inner-city elementary schools. *American Educational Research Journal, 30,* 123–148.

U.S. Department of Education. (1997a). Elementary and secondary education: Fiscal year 1998 budget summary [On-line]. http://www.ed.gov.

U.S. Department of Education. (1997b). America Reads Challenge: President Clinton's call to action for American education in the 21st century [On-line]. http://www.ed.gov.

Wasik, B. (1997) Volunteer tutoring programs: Do we know what works? *Phi Delta Kappan, 79*(4), 282–288

CHAPTER 2

The Role of the Volunteer Coordinator

Getting Set Up

The success of a volunteer tutorial depends on the guidance and support of a knowledgeable coordinator, supervisor, team leader, or manager who tends to the organizational aspects of running an effective tutorial. Such a leader should know something about teaching young children to read, and about how other successful volunteer tutorials have managed. Ideally, the coordinator should have a background in reading education.

Volunteer tutors depend on having a prepared environment. A prepared environment includes a suitable working space, regular routines, ready materials, and appropriate lesson plans to follow. These details must be organized in advance to ensure the volunteers' success. Volunteer tutors also depend on feedback, support, and ongoing guidance as they encounter new and different challenges in the learning-to-read process. This support must be available throughout the duration of the tutorial. Finally, volunteer tutors need to know they are making a difference. They need to know their efforts are paying off.

This chapter describes what must be done before, during, and after volunteers commit their time and energy to teaching a young child to read. The first part of the chapter defines the process of collaborating with school personnel to determine which children would benefit from a volunteer tutorial and how to schedule their tutorials. The second part of the chapter lists the books, supplies, and materials needed to "set up shop." We present our recommended plan for organizing the books for optimal use, and how to manage other materials such as word banks, picture cards, and record forms. The third part of the chapter describes how a coordinator might go about writing individualized lesson plans and how to organize books and materials for individual tutor–tutee pairs. The last part of the chapter outlines recommended practices for modeling instructional procedures and providing feedback for the volunteers. The chapter concludes with recommendations for how to give kudos and rewards to our most valuable resource, our volunteer tutors of emergent and early readers.

Whom to Tutor?

Deciding which children would best be served through a volunteer tutorial is somewhat complex and varies from school to school. One thing is certain: *This is a decision that can not be made alone.* The volunteer coordinator must collaborate with school personnel to make these important decisions. Every school division has rules and regulations for screening volunteers and for obtaining parental permission for children to participate in a volunteer tutorial, and these regulations must be heeded. A sample parent letter and permission form are found in Appendix B.

Many schools have their own means of identifying children at risk for reading failure, particularly in schools served by Title I, a federally funded program for remedial readers. If your school is a Title I school, you might sit down with whoever oversees the Title I referrals and go over the referral list together. Often, these lists are rank-ordered by need, as determined by the school's assessment procedures. In most situations, there will be more children on the referral list than the school has resources to serve. If your volunteer tutorial occurs during the school day, the two of you can negotiate which children would best be served by a reading specialist, and which children would best be served by a volunteer. If your volunteer tutorial occurs as an after-school program, the children might receive both Title I *and* one-on-one tutoring from an after-school volunteer.

Another way to select which children to tutor is simply to ask individual teachers which of their students could use extra help. After getting the referral list from each teacher, the coordinator assesses them all for specific literacy needs, then decides how many and which ones to take. Although this method is simple and straightforward, it lacks the larger vision of the whole-school picture. Ideally, a volunteer tutorial should fit into a school's overall plan for ensuring that all children learn to read.

However the children to be tutored are selected, the total number of tutor–tutee pairs a volunteer coordinator can supervise depends on how many hours the volunteer coordinator can work. As a general rule of thumb, count up the total number of tutoring hours per week and divide it in half. That number will be the total number of hours it will take the coordinator to make lesson plans for the week. For example, if 15 children are to be tutored for 1 hour, two times per week, the total number of tutoring hours would be 30. It would take the coordinator half of those hours (15) to plan for those 30 tutorials. Of course, the coordinator has other responsibilities too, and these also take time, so the number of children to be selected should be carefully planned.

Once the pool of children is identified, the volunteer coordinator will begin to assess each child one-on-one. (The assessment is described in Chapter 3.) How many children are assessed depends on the targeted caseload. In most situations, coordinators can expect to assess more children than will actually be served. If a coordinator anticipates a caseload of 12, for example, it is likely that he or she will assess 15–18 children before determining the final dozen. Children not selected for the tutorial might be placed on a waiting list, or might be served through another program. In any case, it is important that the coordinator or team leader who writes the lesson plans do the assessments. There is no substitute for sitting down next to a child to explore systematically what he or she knows about letters and sounds, about stories and print, and about other important literacy skills. The coordinator is better prepared to write individualized lesson plans for specific children when he or she knows exactly what each child knows about these important literacy fundamentals.

Scheduling Tutorials

Once the children are assessed and selected, the coordinator must go about the business of setting up the tutoring schedule. This process is much easier if the tutorial is set up to be an after-school program. If the volunteer tutorial is designed as an in-school tutorial, the process is more complex. In the latter case, the first step is to get each teacher's schedule. The second step is to find out when each child is available. The third step is to find out when volunteers can come, and to match up the two sets of schedules.

There are two important variables to keep in mind in scheduling tutorials. First is the number of tutorials per week. Research has determined that two times per week is the minimum number of tutoring sessions that will actually make a difference. Fewer than two just doesn't have a prayer of accelerating children's learning. Second is the number of tutors to be supervised at one time. The coordinator's feedback and guidance is essential to the success of a volunteer tutorial. To make that feedback possible, the number of simultaneous tutorials must be kept small—no more than five or six. The fewer tutorials occurring simultaneously, the more attention the coordinator can give to those tutorials as they are occurring. For this reason, it is best to schedule one group of volunteers as a Monday–Wednesday tutorial, and another group of volunteers as a Tuesday–Thursday tutorial. Fridays are good for making up missed sessions due to student or volunteer absence. Volunteers should be instructed from the outset to make up missed sessions so that every child gets at least two tutoring sessions per week.

Acquiring and Organizing Books and Reading Material

Access to lots of books is essential to the success of a volunteer tutorial. One emergent reader who gets tutored twice per week for 7 or 8 months reads anywhere from 50 to 100 books in the tutorial setting alone. If other children are being tutored simultaneously, multiple copies of the same books are a must. There are two major sources of books for emergent and early readers: (1) series books that already come leveled by the publisher, and (2) trade books that the coordinator must level. Trade books may be found in children's bookstores and in libraries. Series books, trade books, and other sources of reading materials are discussed below.

Books for Emergent Readers

Series books for emergent readers are usually "little books" such as the *Ready Readers* published by Modern Curriculum Press, the *Story Box* and *Sunshine Readers* by the Wright Group, the *Little Red Readers* by Sundance, and the *PM Readers* and *Literacy 2000* series by Rigby. Most of the "little books" available from publishers come already organized by level of difficulty. Be sure to ask for the leveling guide, however, because it is not always included with the book order. A list of publishers is found in Appendix B.

Trade books for emergent readers include "easy" books written by popular children's authors such as Raffi, Nancy Tafuri, Brian Wildsmith, or Pat Hutchins. These books may be found in the school and public libraries or in children's bookstores. Information about their level of difficulty is not available on the books themselves, but a leveled list of trade books written by well-known children's authors may be found in Appendix B. Trade books must be leveled by the volunteer coordinator.

Other reading material for emergent readers can be created by the tutors themselves. Children can tell about experiences they have had, and the tutor can write these down, verbatim, as the child speaks. These "dictated experience stories" can be made into little books, and can serve as additional reading material. Nursery rhymes, jump-rope jingles, and other "public domain" rhymes and ditties can be typed up, photocopied, and pasted into "personal readers" that can be read, reread, and sent home. The classroom teacher or a resource teacher who works with the child might also supply reading materials from time to time.

Books for Early Readers

You can still get series books from publishers for early readers, as described earlier, but there is a greater variety of books they can read. Early readers can use easy-to-read trade books such as the *All Aboard Reading, I Can Read, Hello Reader,* or *Step into Reading* series found in many bookstores as well as in the public library. These series are leveled, although the criteria may vary among publishers. In addition to series books, early readers enjoy picture books by authors such as Frank Asch, David McPhail, and Mercer Mayer. These trade books provide reading staples that can be found in the school and public libraries (see Appendix B). Children's poetry collections by Lee Bennett Hopkins and Carl Withers, as well as poetry by Jack Prelutsky, Shel Silverstein, and Eloise Greenfield, provide delightful, easy reading. As children progress in their reading, they will also enjoy non-fiction materials such as the picture captions in *Your Big Backyard,* a magazine published by the National Wildlife Federation. Publishers such as Children's Press, Wright Group, and Rigby, as well as others, have information books especially written for early readers. A favorite science information series is the *Let's Read and Find Out* series, which comes in several different levels of reading difficulty. Of course, early readers can already read preprimer material, so stories from the basal reader used in children's classrooms provide another resource.

Organizing Books for Instruction

Whatever the source of your reading materials, it is absolutely critical to organize these materials in advance by levels. We recommend that the books be grouped and separated by common phonics elements in addition to gradations of reading difficulty. For example, Laura, a volunteer coordinator in the Charlottesville Book Buddies Tutorial, color codes each book by level of difficulty by sticking a colored dot in the top right-hand corner of each book with a number indicating reading level. Each color represents a particular range of difficulty (e.g., levels 7–9 might all have a yellow dot). Laura organizes her little books in plastic tubs that she keeps on a table in the tutoring room. The books inside the tubs are separated by tall cardboard dividers labeled by the phonics elements recurring in all the books between that cardboard divider and the next one. Books that feature beginning consonant sounds such as "b" (*One Bee Got on the Bus* by Ashley Dennis), are separated from books in which a particular rhyming pattern reoccurs (*Cat on the Mat* by Brian Wildsmith). The "phonics ladder" showing the developmental progress of phonics categories is shown in Table 2.1. The most important thing, however, is to organize the book by reading levels, so that each child can read *many* books on their own level.

Since publishers use many different coding systems for book leveling, Table 2.2 cross-references several of the more common "codes" for your convenience. Book titles from Modern Curriculum Press (*Ready Readers*), the Wright Group (*Story Box*), Rigby (*Literacy 2000*), and others are categorized by predominant phonic features and by level of difficulty in Appendix B. A leveled list of trade books, written by well-known children's authors and found in many school and public libraries, is also found in Appendix B.

Organizing your books in this way serves two important purposes. First, the books are organized for instruction in both phonics and reading. The organization forms a curriculum for phonics instruction and, at the same time, a developmental progression of reading difficulty. By pacing the volunteers through this scope and sequence, team leaders can be assured that children will be exposed to the phonics features they need to know and, at the same time, get lots of practice reading at appropriate levels of difficulty. Second, the book organiza-

TABLE 2.1. Phonics Ladder

1. Beginning consonant sounds
2. Beginning consonant blends and digraphs
3. Short vowel rhyming families
4. Short vowel sounds
5. Long and short vowel sounds

TABLE 2.2 The "Reading Ladder"

Reading Recovery levels	*Ready Readers* stages	Basal reader grade levels
1–5	0	Readiness
3–4	0–1	Preprimer 1
5–6	1	Preprimer 2
7–8	2	Preprimer 3
9–12	2, 3, and 4	Primer (1.1)
13–16	3, 4, and 5	Grade 1 (1.2)
17–20	5	Grade 2.1

tion lends itself to efficient planning. If a volunteer coordinator is supervising 12–15 tutor–tutees, that's 30 tutoring lessons the coordinator must write each week. Not only must lessons be written, but the materials must be preselected before the volunteer arrives to tutor. Organizing the books by phonics elements *and by gradations of difficulty* makes this process much more efficient. The books are at the coordinator's fingertips, ready to be matched to the needs of each individual child. How to determine exactly what level book a child should read is described in Chapter 3. Once the initial level is determined, children should have plenty of opportunity to read many books on that level before advancing to the next. How fast the child advances through the levels is determined by the ease or difficulty with which the child is able to read the book. This topic is also discussed in Chapter 3.

Organizing Materials for Word Study and Phonics

Word Banks

As the children learn to read these little books, they will gather the words they know for future word study. Known words can be collected in a "word bank," which is a collection of known words written on small cards to use for phonics and word study. Word-bank work is an important part of the emergent reader lesson plan. Thinking ahead to how this word bank might be organized will add to the efficiency of the tutorial.

Gathering Words for the Word Bank. Word-bank words come from the little books that the children have read and reread. The words are taken out of context to be examined in all their glory, all by themselves. Only words a child recognizes immediately, out of context, are fair game for a word bank. The challenge for the coordinator is how to facilitate this process while allowing for individual differences in which words "stick." One way to plan ahead for gathering word-bank words is to place library pockets in the back of each little book. We recommend the short kind of library pocket so the word cards can easily be stored and retrieved without getting stuck down inside the pocket. The 2½-inch pocket can be ordered from Demco or Hammet school supply catalogues. Figure 2.1 illustrates the placement of the pocket in the back of the book.

Once the library pockets have been glued to the back of the books, the coordinator can pick 6–10 words from the book, print them clearly on blank flash-

FIGURE 2.1. Book with pocket of words.

cards, and place the cards inside the library pockets. Most of the words to be chosen should exemplify the phonics feature being taught. Other words might be high-frequency words such as "from" or "with," or interesting content words such as "snake." In reviewing the book *One Bee Got on the Bus*, for example, Laura, a coordinator in the Book Buddies program, chose the following words to print on word cards for the library pocket: "bats," "bug," "bear," "bus," "bee," and "buzz" (which targeted the letter sound for "b") and "on," "got," and "the" (which are common high-frequency words). All nine words were printed in perfect first-grade-teacher print onto word cards, which were placed in the library pockets in the back of the book.

The advanced preparation involved in preparing word cards in library pockets in the back of each book will pay off later as volunteer tutors work with individual children. After rereading several familiar books, the tutor can lay out the word cards from the back of the last book and ask the child to pick up the words he or she knows. A record of these words can be made on the alphabetic word-bank record form (see Appendix A) then copied onto blank word cards for the child's own word bank. The book's word cards are returned to the library pocket in the back of the book for use by other students who will read that book at a different time.

Organizing the Words in the Word Banks.   After planning ahead for the process of gathering word-bank words, volunteer coordinators can begin to think about where individual word cards will be kept and how best to organize them for instructional purposes. There are many different ways to store individual word-bank words, ranging from small plastic zip-lock bags to herbal tea boxes. Almost any storage container will do. However, for optimal use in instruction, word-bank words must be organized, and the way they are organized will change as the child learns more and more about the way words are spelled.

Once again, we recommend library pockets. This time, the library pockets are glued onto two joined manila folders which, when taped on one edge, form a four-fold, desktop pocket chart such as that shown in Figure 2.2. Library pockets can be labeled by the phonics features being taught. Since these features will change as the child progresses, we advise the volunteer team leader to assemble

FIGURE 2.2. Word-bank pocket folder by beginning sounds.

several word-bank folders that correspond to the phonics categories used to organized the books. For emergent readers, this will most likely be by initial sounds. As children progress in their reading and spelling, their word-bank words may be reorganized by word families or vowel sounds.

Picture Cards for Phonics Sorts

A routine part of the lesson plan for both emergent and early readers involves phonics instruction using picture cards. Picture cards for phonics instruction must be organized ahead of time so that tutors may have easy access to the sound cards they need. Picture cards may be bought from most teacher supply stores, or photocopied from *Words Their Way* by Bear, Invernizzi, Templeton, and Johnston (1996). A complete set of picture cards for phonics sorts may also be ordered using the form in Appendix B. Photocopying these picture cards onto cardstock makes them easier to pick up and move. Once the picture cards are copied, laminated (optional), and cut, they can be organized by the scope and sequence of phonics features to be taught as categorized in the "phonics ladder" (Table 2.1).

There are several possible ways to organize the picture cards within these phonics categories. Coordinators might store picture cards in empty flashcard boxes, separating the pictures by a larger piece of cardboard inserted between categories. This larger piece of cardboard can serve as a label for each phonics category. A particularly useful way to organize the picture cards is to use, once again, library pockets. However, unlike the library pockets used for word-bank words, these library pockets are not glued down. Rather, picture cards are stored in freestanding library pockets that are labeled according to the sounds the pictures represent. Organized in this fashion, a volunteer tutor can simply grab the library pockets labeled by the phonics features to be taught, shuffle them all together, then have the child sort them under the spelling pattern that labels each pocket. After the picture sort, the pictures are shuffled, returned to their pocket, and then placed in the box. Of course, it is the coordinator's job to

FIGURE 2.3. "Push It Say It" cards.

tell the tutor which phonics features to compare and contrast, and this is determined by the assessment described in the next chapter.

Letter Cards for "Push It Say It" Activities

Phonics instruction for the emergent and early reader concludes with a brief "Push It Say It" activity designed to provide concrete, explicit practice with dividing a word into individual sounds and matching letters to each sound. These activities are described in the word-study component of the lesson plan in Chapter 4.

Letter cards for "Push It Say It" can be copied from Appendix A or written on small cards and stored with the pictures described earlier. You might store the beginning consonant cards and the vowel chunk cards in library pockets labeled with the word that the letter cards will make, as shown in Figure 2.3. Some coordinators glue a library pocket on one side of the two-pocket folder that every tutor has in his or her tutoring box (see Figure 2.4, and "Organizing the Tutoring Box," below). "Push It Say It" letter cards can be tucked inside this pocket and exchanged on a lesson-by-lesson basis.

FIGURE 2.4. Two-pocket folder for lesson plan and materials.

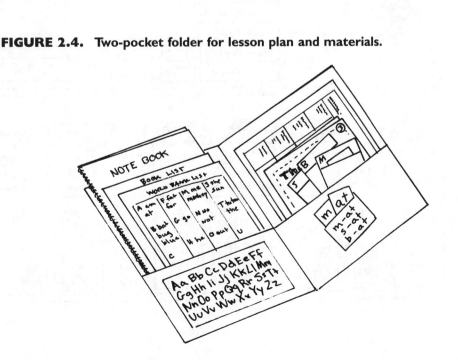

Word Cards

Although much of the word study for emergent readers will be done with pictures and word-bank words, a collection of word cards by phonics features will be needed for the early reader. There are two ways you might prepare these:

1. Words may be written on cards and stored in the same manner as the picture cards.

2. Words may be written on the word template in Appendix A, copied, and cut apart by the coordinator or the tutor. The original copy can be stored to use again.

Word lists by phonic features can be found in Chapter 5. Additional words should come from the child's reading materials.

Organizing General Supplies and Record Forms

Books, library pockets, and word, picture, and letter cards are the five most critical instructional materials to organize. Other supplies and materials should also be organized in advance, though the method for organizing these depend on the time and space available for tutoring. It might be prudent to organize one spot for "communal supplies," which all volunteer tutors will have to "dip into" on a daily basis. Among these, the most used would be general supplies, boxes of flashcards, alphabet cards, and record forms (see Figure 2.5).

General supplies that might go into the communal area include a variety of papers, pencils, scissors, stick-on notes, and other desk supplies. Boxes of blank

FIGURE 2.5. Tutoring supply center.

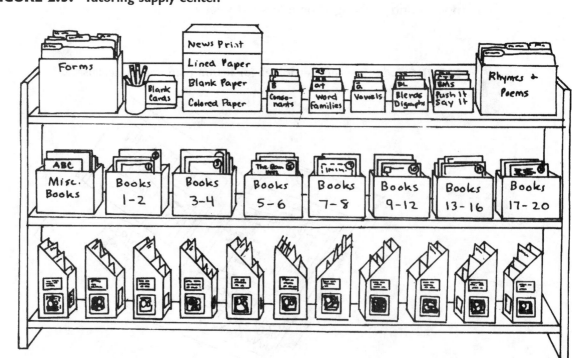

flashcards can be purchased through most teacher supply catalogues and cost between $3 and $5 for a box of a thousand. Simply place a box of these cards in the communal supply area for tutors to use to make word cards. Alphabet letters (magnetic letters, tiles, link letters, or paper letter cards) are especially useful for teaching emergent readers who have incomplete knowledge of the alphabet.

Copies of various record forms must also be readily available, organized in folders in a box. Word-bank record forms and "Books I Have Read" forms are heavily used. Other helpful forms include sound boards (pictures clues for letter sounds) and handwriting sheets that include arrows for letter formation. All of these may be found in Appendix A. If books are sent home for practice, a checkout-and-return form must be created.

Writing Lesson Plans

The most important job of the volunteer coordinator or team leader is to write the daily lesson plans for individual children. In addition, the coordinator needs to gather the books and materials to go with the plan. Tutors appreciate being able to arrive shortly before a session, pick up a prepared box of materials, quickly read through the lesson plan, then sit down and work with their child.

The lesson plans described in Chapters 4 and 5 are both four-part plans representing a balanced literacy diet. The emergent plan includes (1) rereading familiar texts, (2) word study (word-bank work, alphabet, and phonics), (3) writing, and (4) learning to read new texts. The early reader plan, for children who can already read preprimer material, is also a four-part plan and includes (1) reading familiar or easy materials, (2) reading and writing, (3) word study, and (4) revisiting a favorite book. Most of what a child needs to know about reading, writing, and spelling can be incorporated into these four-part plans.

The four-part lesson plan for both the emergent and early readers entails critical decision making on the part of the coordinator or team leader. For example, in order to reread familiar or easy materials (Part I of the lesson plan), the coordinator must know what an individual child can and cannot read, what's easy and what's difficult. This information can be obtained from the assessments described in Chapter 3. Likewise, in order to know what letter sounds or phonics/spelling features to target during word study (Part II of the lesson plan), the coordinator must know which letters and letter sounds an individual child already knows, and which he or she still needs to learn. Again, the answer lies in each child's assessment. Finally, to plan an appropriate writing activity (Part III of the lesson plan) for a particular child, the coordinator must know what the child can write and what he or she needs to practice. This information, too, will be found in each child's assessment.

By now, it is easy to see that the assessment information is absolutely necessary for the coordinator to write meaningful lesson plans. Keep the assessment handy to refer to when making plans, and then use the activities described in Chapters 4 and 5 to meet individual needs. Copies of a tutoring plan for either the emergent or the early readers can be found in Appendix A.

Organizing the Tutoring Box

A simple means of organizing a particular child's tutoring lesson is to gather all the books and materials and put them in a box. We recommend using "Darby boxes" similar to the boxes in libraries to store periodicals (except that they store materials vertically rather than horizontally, see Figure 2.6). Darby boxes can be ordered from most teacher supply catalogues. Lesson plans and other loose sheets of paper, such as the "Word-Bank Record Form" and the "Books I Have Read" form, can be easily kept in a two-pocket folder, placing lesson plans in one pocket and record forms in the other.

The Emergent Reader Tutoring Box

Within each box, the following items should be placed:

1. Five or six familiar books for rereading. These should be books the child has read before in the previous five or six tutorials. These books should already have library pockets in the back, with appropriate word cards.

2. A two-pocket folder (Figure 2.4) containing:
   a. The lesson plan.
   b. "Books I Have Read " form. This ongoing record is updated regularly to provide positive feedback.
   c. A "Word-Bank Record" form for recording known words.
   d. A handwriting guide for letter formation.
   e. Alphabet record form, if needed.

3. The word-bank folder for organizing word-bank words.

4. Picture cards for alphabet and phonics instruction. These may be placed in small plastic bags, secured with rubber bands, or transported in their library pockets as described earlier.

5. A notebook for writing letters, words, and sentences. This may be a wide-ruled composition book, a stapled booklet made from primary newsprint, or ordinary wide-ruled notebook paper.

7. A new book to be introduced and read for the first time that session.

8. Two pencils.

9. Blank word cards.

Occasionally the coordinator may also want to include an alphabet, phonics, or word-bank game such as Bingo or Go Fish.

FIGURE 2.6. Individual Darby box.

The Early Reader Tutoring Box

The early reader box must be organized in a similar fashion. A two-pocket folder organizes the lesson plans and record forms. Books and other instructional materials are placed in the box and include the following:

1. Easy reading, poems, or familiar reading material for Part I of the lesson plan.

2. Reading material on the child's current reading level for guided reading.

3. A writing tablet, notebook, or stapled booklet for writing about what is read and for writing word sorts.

4. Picture cards and word cards for phonics sorts.

5. A favorite book to revisit at the end.

6. A two-pocket folder containing:
   a. The lesson plan.
   b. Timed repeated reading forms.
   c. A "Books I Have Read" form.
   d. A handwriting guide.

7. Two pencils.

These materials should be organized within the box and folder to help indicate what goes together with what and for what part of the lesson. If the coordinator has done a good job of planning for instruction, the volunteer tutor should be able to follow the lesson plan expediently with little fumbling about. If the tutoring box looks like a squirrel's nest after the tutorial, the coordinator needs to come up with an immediate solution.

Preparing the Outside of the Tutoring Box

The outside of the Darby boxes will require some advance preparation too. Sound boards and alphabet strips should all be glued to the outside of the Darby box for ready reference as needed. Emergent readers will frequently need to consult an alphabet strip to remember how to write a particular letter. Which sound board you glue on the outside of the box will depend on where each child is on the phonics ladder. If a child is learning beginning sounds, glue a beginning sound board to the outside of the box. If a child is learning consonant blends, glue a consonant blend sound board to the box. Alphabet strips and sound boards may be found in Appendix A.

The finishing touch in preparing tutoring boxes is to personalize each box with the name of the volunteer tutor and the name of the child on the side. A Polaroid picture of the two of them at work can also be added. It also helps to put the days and times the volunteer tutor comes to work with the child on the side of the box. Equipped accordingly, the volunteer tutors can come in, grab their boxes, read through the lesson plan, and easily tell what materials go with what part of the lesson. Of course, the tutor must also know *how* to conduct each part of this four-part plan. Recommendations for teaching volunteer tutors *how* to tutor and for modeling and providing ongoing support and guidance are outlined below.

Volunteer Tutor Training

The training of volunteer tutors is an ongoing process. Although it is helpful to have a whole-group training session before the tutoring begins, these initial large-group sessions do little more that provide the big picture of what the tutoring looks like and what it involves. Whole-group training sessions cannot teach volunteers all they need to know. Nevertheless, big pictures are important. Volunteers need to know what they are getting into and what is expected. Whole-group training sessions can set the tone for the tutoring program and outline goals and expectations. For this reason, it is best to begin with a whole-group training session, with one caveat: Don't be deluded into thinking that this will be enough. Volunteer tutors, like the children they will tutor, learn best on the job, one-on-one. Recommended practices for training volunteers on the job, throughout the year, will be described after a discussion of whole-group training.

Whole-Group Training Sessions

The best way to give volunteer tutors an idea of what is involved in a reading tutorial is to use videotapes of actual tutoring sessions. An order form for a videotape of the emergent lesson plan may be found in Appendix B. Volunteers can follow the video using a written lesson plan as a road map for viewing. It is a good idea to have a leader who starts and stops the tape and facilitates a discussion of what's going on in each part of the lesson. Since the lesson is divided into four parts, it is logical to stop the videotape at the end of each part to summarize what was done and why. The leader may ask volunteers to look for certain behaviors prior to starting the tape again, thus giving them a purpose for viewing. The volunteers should be referred to specific pages in the tutoring manual for more information about each part. The more interactive the videotape viewing, the more the volunteers will get out of the group training session. Other ideas for interactive video follow.

Ideas for Video Training

1. Volunteers can fill in the "comments" section of a lesson plan after viewing each part on the video. Use the questions at the end of each lesson plan section in Chapters 4 and 5 to prompt specific observational notes. These comments can be shared and compared.

2. Volunteers can practice each part of the lesson plan with a partner sitting next to them. Team leaders can circulate to model and provide feedback as they observe the volunteers teaching each other. Of course, this idea would require planning for enough tutoring books and materials to go around.

3. Volunteers can be shown the reading "ladder," a basal reading series laid out in sequential order from the Preprimer A through the second- or third-grade reader. Corresponding "little books" can be laid out beneath each reader so the tutors can see the increments in difficulty between levels. It is important for volunteers to know the terrain they will be traveling.

4. Volunteers can be shown the "phonics ladder" (Table 2.1), the sequence of phonics features to be learned. Again, it is important for volunteers to know the domain of what is to be learned, and know that there is an orderly progression for instruction. It might also be helpful to lay out specific goals related to both "ladders." Yearly goals for emergent readers might include the following:

   a. To read approximately 60–80 books and poems.

   b. To recognize all 26 letters of the alphabet, upper and lower case, and to produce each letter.

   c. To know the sound each letter represents and to apply that knowledge in decoding new words and in writing.

   d. To fingerpoint accurately while reading a known story.

   e. To use accurately in writing:
      (1) All consonants.
      (2) Long vowel *sounds* (but *not* necessarily the silent markers such as the silent "e" at the end of rake).
      (3) Short vowel sounds.
      (4) Consonant blends (*bl*ue, *bl*ack, *bl*ob) and consonant digraphs (*sh*eep, *sh*ip, *sh*oe).

   f. To recognize immediately 100+ words from the word bank.

Addressing Issues and Questions

Another purpose for providing a whole-group volunteer training session before the tutoring begins is to address educational issues within the community. A question we often get from volunteers is why we allow children to make spelling errors in their writing. Most laypeople do not understand the role of spelling in learning to read, and this politically charged issue needs to be addressed head-on. Once volunteers have seen the "ladder" of phonics and spelling features to be learned, it is easy for them to understand that these features progress from easier one (letters and individual letter sounds) to harder ones (silent letters marking the long vowel sound). The answer to the question "When do we start holding them accountable for correct spelling?" is this: Right from the start. We hold children accountable for what they've been taught, but we ignore their mistakes on features further along on the phonics ladder. This rule of thumb means we *do* correct children when they make an error on a phonics or spelling feature they have been taught, but we do *not* penalize them for what they haven't yet been taught. No double jeopardy allowed! A little bit of knowledge can go a long way toward unpacking unfounded political rhetoric, and whole-group training sessions can provide a little bit of knowledge. And every little bit helps.

Procedures and Rules for Tutors

Whole-group training sessions might also give information on procedures for checking into the school building, rules for making up missed tutoring sessions due to illness, vacation or other interference, and general tips for tutoring (see below). It is useful to stress the following points in a whole-group situation:

Rules for Tutors	■ Regular attendance is critical. Children look forward to seeing their tutors and are disappointed when they do not appear. Missed sessions should be made up.
	■ Come prepared. Tutors should come a few minutes before the time they are scheduled to begin working with their child in order to go over the day's plan. The tutoring session should be paced so that little time is wasted.
	■ Be friendly but firm. Tutors and students must abide by school rules, such as no running and no gum chewing. Volunteer tutors should abide by school regulations themselves. Tutors should not bring food, drinks, or gum to a tutoring session.
	■ Be patient. Beginners need time to figure things out and master them. Tutors should not be too quick to correct a mistake. Students should be given a chance to discover their mistake first—they will learn much more from the experience.
	■ Reward hard work and success with praise. Tutors should encourage their students and maintain a positive atmosphere. However, tutors should avoid treats such as candy or presents unless it is a special occasion.

■ Seek help. Working with young children is not always easy. Encourage volunteers to seek help when they have questions and problems. Most of the time, the coordinator can provide all the help and guidance that is needed, but sometimes other school personnel may be needed. Teachers, librarians, and school guidance counselors are there to help.

Further Training

Whole-group training sessions can provide a general orientation, but they are no substitute for lessons learned on the job. Ongoing tutor training must happen on-site, continuously, throughout the year. Practices for modeling and providing feedback throughout the tutorial are described below.

The First Session

The scariest point for the tutors is probably the first time they meet their child, so you should talk about this in one of the training sessions. During most sessions, tutors are encouraged to maintain a steady pace and to keep the child's attention on the tasks to be accomplished, but the very first session may be more relaxed—an opportunity for the volunteer tutor to get to know his or her student and vice versa. Here are some suggestions for that first meeting:

Suggestions for the First Tutorial

■ Tutors might share something about themselves—a favorite hobby, family pets, and so on. Children, in turn, are asked to share something about their family as well. Some volunteer tutoring programs take pictures of the tutors and their children, and put them up on the bulletin board with "All about Me" blurbs under each photograph.

■ Tutors might bring something from home that reveals their interests and engage the child, such as photographs, a collection, a memento from a trip, and so on.

■ Tutors should talk about why they will be coming to work with their child. They should be clear that the goal of their time together is to learn to read better, but they should be cautioned not to make promises that they can't keep.

■ Tutors might bring a favorite book to read aloud.

On-Site Modeling and Feedback

The ideal way to teach volunteers how to tutor is to have them observe the coordinator or team leader conduct the first formal lesson with their child. Thereafter, the volunteers can be "weaned" into independence one part, or one half, of the lesson plan at a time.

Once a volunteer tutor is up and running, it is essential that the coordinator be on hand for at least part of each tutorial to stay in touch. Only by keeping in touch with the details of how things are going can the coordinator jump in and model where needed, or coach the tutor after the tutorial session. Of course, this is impossible if too many tutorials are scheduled simultaneously. The maximum number of tutor–tutee pairs a coordinator can effectively supervise at *one time* is about six (see previous section on scheduling).

Even with optimal scheduling, however, its is not humanly possible to tune into the details of six tutorials simultaneously. The coordinator's attention will shift from pair to pair during different parts of the lesson. Because of this, the coordinator must rely on the tutor's comments written in the comment section of the lesson plan. These comments provide feedback to the coordinator as to how things went and help to fill in the gaps of what was not observed. These comments are essential in planning the next day's lesson. Taken together, the coordinator's observations and the volunteer tutor's comments will begin to shape the direction of the tutorial.

Tutor's Common Concerns

Some issues that require the coordinator's feedback and guidance are common to many volunteer tutorials. Tutors frequently worry about their child's reluctance to read or write. Some volunteers may end up with an uncooperative child, and this can be a frustrating experience for everyone. Volunteers may feel strongly about reading to children, even if "reading to" had not been a planned part of the tutorial. Volunteer coordinators can anticipate these issues and be prepared to give helpful feedback. Some common concerns and suggested words of wisdom are discussed below.

My Child Is Reluctant to Read!   Reluctance to read may be due to several different causes: lack of ownership, frustration, lack of confidence, or boredom. Tutors should offer their student a structured choice among a limited number of alternatives. Asking "What would you like to read first?" among a set of alternatives might be all that is needed to give the child a sense of ownership and control. It may be that the material is too difficult and you need to reassess what you are asking the child to read. If a child is missing more than one word in 10, the book is probably too hard, and easier material is in order. It may be that the child still lacks confidence in his or her own ability. The tutor can provide more support by reading with the child, reading every other page ("I'll read a page, and then you read a page"), or echo reading ("I'll read this first and then you read it after me"). However, this should be done only as long as it seems absolutely necessary. The point of rereading familiar material is for the child to read independently, without support. Finally, the child may be bored with the same old routine, or the same old story. Try varying the order of the lesson plan, and try switching roles. The tutor becomes the "child" and the child becomes the "teacher." The tutor reads slowly, asks the child for help, and makes mistakes the child can correct. In this role, tutors can sound out words for the child, who must guess what the word may be.

My Child Is Not Cooperating!   Tutors sometimes have difficulty keeping their child's attention. We have found the following techniques to be helpful:

1. Never ask the child a question for which he or she can say "No!" Rather than saying "Do you want to read now?" say "Now we will read. Which book do you want to read first?" Rather than saying "Do you want to write now?" say "Now we will write. Do you want to use a pencil or a pen?" *You* must decide what is to be done during the tutoring, but you can give the child choices within each component of the lesson plan.

2. Keep up a brisk pace. A forward momentum helps keep the child engaged in the lesson. To keep moving along, however, tutors must come to the tutorial prepared. In addition, tutors should avoid getting sidetracked. Interesting but irrelevant conversations should be saved for the end of the tutorial.

3. Keep the tutoring routine the same, so that the child knows what to expect during each tutoring session. Routines provide the structure and security that young children often need. Tutors can prepare their student for what comes next in the lesson by making comments such as, "This will be the last book that we will read, and then we will look at your word-bank words."

4. Involve the student in the management of the lesson. Tutors should include the student in clerical tasks such as coloring in the word-bank rocket , reciting the spelling of words as they are recorded on the word-bank record form, and so on. Students can help put word cards away and take part in other housekeeping details.

5. Provide a simplified lesson plan for the child. You might use an index card with items for the child to check off as he completes the task. This makes the child feel in control of his own learning. An example can be seen in Figure 2.7.

6. Avoid negative feedback. When a child makes a mistake, rather than saying "No," ask questions that lead her to the correct answer (for example, "Let's look at that again," or "What would make sense?" or "What do you see in this picture?").

FIGURE 2.7. Simplified lesson plan for the child.

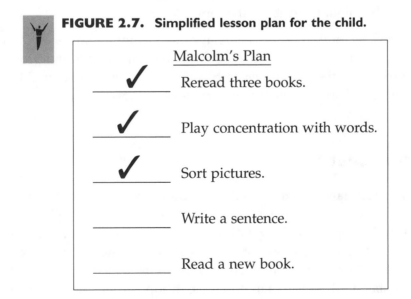

Malcolm's Plan

✔ _____ Reread three books.

✔ _____ Play concentration with words.

✔ _____ Sort pictures.

_____ Write a sentence.

_____ Read a new book.

7. Avoid criticizing the child. If a child engages in annoying behavior, criticize the action specifically, but do not criticize the child. For example, if the child is whining, the tutor might say, "Don't go whining on me; I hate whining!" Specific comments such as this indicate it's the "whining" that is disliked, not the child.

8. Establish and maintain boundaries. Children need to know what is expected (that is, that they will be following the lesson plan and what constitutes acceptable behavior). Children need to know who is in charge.

What about Reading to My Child?   Reading books aloud to children is a very important part of any reading program. It has not been included in the lesson plans described in Chapters 4 and 5 because the time allotted for tutoring is short. We are assuming that the classroom teacher provides this experience regularly. However, if you sense that your student has had few experiences with books, then it may be a worthwhile to read aloud as the very last activity, or as a reward for a child's hard work. If there is time to read aloud, select books that can be read in a short amount of time (about 5 minutes). Include information books to expand the child's vocabulary and world knowledge.

The emphasis in read alouds is upon the children enjoying the book as they listen and look at the illustrations. Here are a few suggestions to give to tutors:

1. Look at the cover, point out and read the title, and ask the child to make some predictions about what the book will be about. Discuss the book's author and illustrator.

2. Encourage the child to respond to the book with questions and comments.

3. Elaborate on the content of the book to enhance the child's understanding. Tutors might explain unfamiliar words and point out interesting details in the pictures.

4. Talk briefly about the book after reading it. Tutors might ask the child about her favorite part, whether she has had a related experience, or other questions she might have about the topic.

These are some of the concerns we have heard from volunteer tutors year after year. As volunteer coordinators model the tutoring process and provide feedback throughout the year, other problems and concerns are bound to appear. These must be handled one by one, on a case-by-case basis.

Kudos for Our Volunteers

Volunteer tutorials capitalize on the human resources inherent within every community; concerned citizens of all ages. These volunteers give their time and talents in the hope of making a difference. They truly want to save the world.

We all have a vested interest in having our volunteers return from one year to the next. Most of our volunteers become quite skilled over time, and the training described in this chapter, both whole-group and on-site, represents a considerable investment. Our return is proportional to what we put into supporting and rewarding our volunteers. On-the-job praise and encouragement go a long way. Thanks and public acknowledgment go even further. Any of us would gloat over a letter sent to our "boss" singing our praises. We all take pride in being acknowledged in the newspaper, on television or radio. But beyond all this is the real kudo: *progress.*

The best way to give kudos to our most valuable resource is to share the data. Coordinators or team leaders conduct assessments to determine what each child needs to learn (see Chapter 3). These assessments need to be shared with the tutors so they can proceed fully informed as to where they're headed. Coordinators also conduct assessments midyear to gauge progress, and at the end of the year to gauge how far they've come. Data from the assessment summary sheet need to be shared with the tutor at the beginning, the middle, and the end of the tutorial year. The going can be long and tough. But if a tutor can see that a child who knew only two letters in September knows 24 in November, that tutor can see progress. Even if the child does not make it all the way to grade level by the end of the year, the tutor needs to see how far up the ladder he or she climbed. Coordinators or team leaders of volunteer tutorials owe it to their volunteers to share the assessment data. The child's progress is their true reward.

The data from the assessment summary sheet, described in the next chapter, provide the coordinator and the tutor with information about what the child already knows. Chapters 4 and 5 explain how to move the child forward and extend what he or she knows. Good luck!

Reference

Bear, D., Invernizzi, M., Templeton, S., & Johnston, F. (1995). *Words their way: Word study for phonics, spelling and vocabulary development.* Englewood Cliffs, NJ: Merrill.

CHAPTER 3

Evaluating Beginning Readers

This chapter describes how to assess and then how to interpret results in order to evaluate and plan instruction for beginning readers. The assessment described in this chapter is adapted from the Test of Early Word Knowledge used extensively by the McGuffey Reading Center of the University of Virginia and the Early Reading Screening Inventory developed by Darrell Morris (1992). This assessment is designed to be used with beginning readers in first and second grade, or any students who have not yet begun to read with much accuracy. The total assessment takes 30 to 40 minutes and is sometimes administered in two sessions with young children.

These testing materials can be used for the initial assessment, to assess ongoing progress, and as a final assessment for measuring growth at the end of the year. There is space on the Assessment Summary Sheet (Form A, page 45) for all three sets of scores. *Do not use any of these assessment materials for instruction* or they cannot be used for later testing. The assessment tasks are described briefly below. Detailed directions for administering the tasks, and the needed forms and record sheets are included at the end of this chapter. The initial assessment is such a critical aspect of an effective tutoring program that it is best done by the reading coordinator or someone who has experience working with young readers and using similar tests.

An Overview of the Assessment

Before tutoring begins, it is absolutely essential to discover what children already know about reading and how print works. This information will enable you to find reading materials and plan activities that are not too difficult. This chapter describes assessment tasks that will test knowledge of the alphabet, letter–sound knowledge, and identification of words in lists and in stories. Each of these tasks is described briefly below. The directions for administering each task are thoroughly described in the sections that follow.

Alphabet and Letter–Sounds

Familiarity with the letters of the alphabet as well as the sounds associated with those letters (phonics) is essential for learning to read and spell the English language. Alphabet knowledge is assessed for both identification (letter naming) and production (letter writing). Letter naming is tested as students identify both upper- and lowercase letters presented in random order. Production is tested as children write letters called out in random order. Letter–sound knowledge is assessed two different ways. Children are asked to sort a collection of pictures into categories by the beginning sound and then asked to spell 10 words. The spelling task offers information about how completely children are able to separate and attend to the sounds in a word (phonemic awareness) as well as their ability to match those sounds to letters. Results of these assessments are used to plan the word-study portion of the lesson.

Word Identification

There are three parts of the word identification assessment: (1) concept of word, (2) word-list reading, and (3) story reading. Students will have a difficult time learning to read if they cannot locate the words on the page and match their oral speech to the printed words in a line of text. This skill, known as *concept of word*, includes the understanding that print moves from left to right and top to bottom, as well as an understanding of where words begin and end, and how the spaces between words establish word boundaries. Although those words and spaces are very obvious to us, they are not obvious to emergent readers. Concept of word is assessed by asking children to point to the words of a short story that has been read to them. The children repeat the story sentence by sentence, pointing to the words as they say them. In addition, children are asked to identify selected words in the sentences.

To place children in material that they can read with success and understanding, it is necessary to get a good estimate of their reading level. Reading levels can be described in a number of ways. A long-standing system describes beginning readers as being in the readiness, preprimer, primer, or first-grade levels. The *preprimer* levels correspond to early first grade, the *primer* level to middle first grade, and the *first-grade* level to late first grade. Subsequent levels would be second grade, third grade, and so on. In this book, we use the numerical system developed by Reading Recovery® teachers for leveling reading materials. Both of these systems are used in Figure 3.5 (page 42), which will help you place children at an approximate level using the results of the word-list reading and story-reading tasks.

The first word identification task is to simply have children read from a list of preprimer words, primer words, or first-grade words. These lists are a sample of the kinds of words found in many reading materials at those levels. The second task requires children to read aloud several simple stories as you keep a record of the errors they make. The information from these two sources will enable you to get a fairly good estimate of a child's ability to read with success at a particular level or range of levels.

Administering the Assessment

Before you begin the assessment, you should be thoroughly familiar with the procedures described below and get your materials in order.

Before Testing

1. Read over the directions carefully (both those below and those on the individual assessment forms).

2. Make copies of Forms A, B, and C in this chapter (8 pages in all). You will mark on these forms.

3. Make a copy of Form D.2 and cut apart the pictures for sorting.

4. Arrange the materials in the order you will need them.

5. You will need this book and a pen or pencil for recording, as well as a pencil and some paper for the child to use.

6. Arrange for a quiet place to work.

During Testing

1. Set the child at ease by chatting with her briefly and then explain that you are going to ask her to do some reading and writing with you. At all points in the assessment, assure the child that she is doing well and that you do not expect her to know how to do everything perfectly.

2. Start with the alphabet tasks, since these are usually the easiest and children can feel successful. Complete the recording forms.

3. Go on to the picture sorting task and record the results.

4. Call out the spelling words as directed and score at a later time.

5. The word-list reading task needs to be administered next in order to make decisions about the concept of word task and the story-reading tasks. Record errors on the word-list chart.

6. Story reading is the last step and might be saved for a second session, which will enable you to make copies of the stories that you expect to use. Record results on Forms C.3 and C.4.

1. Score the spelling test and any others you have not yet done.

2. Transfer all of the results to the one-page Assessment Summary Sheet (Form A on page 45), which will be used to estimate the child's reading level and plan instruction.

3. Record observations about children's general demeanor and reactions to testing in the space at the bottom of the Assessment Summary Sheet. Were they nervous, confident, talkative, shy, tense, relaxed, and so on?

Alphabet Knowledge Assessment Tasks

This part of the assessment contains two parts: identification and production. You will need a copy of both upper- and lowercase letters in random order (Form D.1, page 53) and the Assessment Recording Form (Form B, page 48). Your child will need a pencil and paper for the production task.

Letter Identification

Show your child the capital and lowercase letters. Say: "See these letters? Put your finger on each letter and name it. If you don't know the name of a letter, skip it and go to the next." On recording Form B, circle any incorrect responses. If children correct themselves immediately, check the circle and count the response as correct. Reversals (such as "b" for "d") are errors. If children take more than 3 seconds to name a letter, count it as an error. They may be reciting the alphabet or using some other means of coming up with a good guess, but they do not really know that letter "by heart." Count up the number of errors, subtract it from 26, and record this number beside each "total" on the recording form.

Letter Production

There are two ways to assess a child's ability to write the alphabet: (1) Call out the letters one by one in the same sequence as listed on Form D.1. (2) Sing the alphabet song *with* the child as he or she writes the letters. Have a sheet of lined or unlined paper available for this task and tell the child, "If you aren't sure how to make a letter, you can skip it." Accept either the capital or the lowercase letter as correct. *Reversals are scored as correct* (for example, "b" for "d") this time. Reversals are common for emergent and early readers, but you should note which ones are causing problems. Record the number of letters produced on the recording Form B.

Letter–Sound Awareness Tasks

The child's knowledge of sounds in words and letter–sound correspondences is assessed in two ways: picture sorting by the beginning sound and by asking the child to spell 10 words.

FIGURE 3.1. Picture sorting task.

Picture Sorting

For this task, you will need the pictures for sorting (see Figure 3.1) that begin with the consonant letters "b," "m," and "s" (Form D.2). Make a copy of page 54 and cut the pictures apart. Pull out the *sun, moon,* and *bug* to use as headers and models. The other pictures should be mixed up. Your directions to the child will go something like this:

> "This is a sun. Ssssun starts with s-s-s-s *(make the sound of 's' and point to the 's' beside the picture of the sun).* You are going to put all the words that start with s-s-s-s under the sun. This is a moon. Mmmmoon starts with m-m-m *(make the sound and point to the 'm' beside the picture of the moon).* You are going to put all the words that start with m-m-m-m under the moon. Here is a bug. Bug starts with b-b-b-b *(repeat the sound several times and point to the 'b' beside the bug).* Put all the pictures that begin with b-b-b-b under the bug."

After modeling this for the child you begin the actual assessment by pulling out another picture and saying something like this:

> "Here is a picture of 'a sock.' Where will you put the sock? Under the sun, the moon, or the bug?"

If the child puts it under the wrong picture, it will count as an error, but model correct placement by saying:

> "S-s-s-sock. The sock will go under the sun. Listen, s-s-s-sock, s-s-s-sun."

Hand your child the rest of the pictures to sort. Correct only the first three efforts. From then on, let pictures fall where they may. Record the number of *unassisted* correct responses on Form B.

Spelling

In this part of the assessment you will call out 10 words for the child to spell as best he can. Make a copy of Form C.1, Spelling Assessment, on page 49. Fold under all but the row of empty boxes on the left side. Children write each word in these blank numbered boxes. Have a copy of the alphabet available (page 133) for reference in case a child is unsure how to write a letter. Some children may be comfortable about attempting the spelling of words they have never written before, but others will not. Before you begin, you should model a sound-it-out strategy by slowly saying the sounds of the sample word "map" and writing it for the child as suggested below:

> "We are going to write the word 'map.' Listen to me say the sounds in 'map': m-m-m-a-a-a-p. What letter should I write down first? This word starts with 'm' *(point to the 'm' in an alphabet strip)*. What letter should I write down next? Now I need the letter 'a'. What do you hear at the end? Listen again, m-m-m-a-a-a-p *(emphasize the 'p')*. I'll end this word with the letter 'p' *(point to it on an alphabet chart)*.
>
> "Now I am going to call out some words for you to spell. Spell them the best way you can. Think about the sounds you hear in the word and the letters you need to write the sound."

You are now ready to call out these words for the child to write.

1. van	3. rug	5. plum	7. shine	9. float
2. pet	4. sad	6. chip	8. skate	10. treat

Pronounce the words clearly and naturally. Repeat them as needed, and use in a sentence. Limit your prompts to "What else do you hear?" *Do not* elongate the sounds of the words as you did in the modeling part. Call out all 10 words unless your child is clearly uncomfortable or is unable to spell even a single letter of the word. If the child asks you if a word is correct, respond by saying, "You are doing a good job listening for the sounds," or "You have most of the letters in that word—good job!" Listen as the child works out the spelling of each word and ask him immediately if you are unsure of what a letter might be. *Reversals on this task will not count as spelling errors* (reversals are generally handwriting errors).

Score the spelling at a later time by checking the appropriate boxes according to the sounds that the child was able to represent correctly or with a logical substitution. For example, the word "van" might have been spelled "fn." (Say "van and "fan" to yourself, and you might "feel" how similar those two consonant sounds are.) The spelling of "fn" for "van" would be worth two points because the child has represented two sounds in the word, the initial and final consonants. A sample test has been scored in Figure 3.2 for you. The Spelling Error Analysis Score Sheet in Figure 3.3 (see page 38) will assist you in deciding if a substitution is similar enough in sound to be a logical and acceptable substitution. Sum the number of points for each word, adding an additional bonus point if the word is spelled correctly. Total the number of points at the bottom of the spelling form, and write that total on the Assessment Summary Sheet A.

The Word Identification Assessment

The word identification part of the assessment consists of three parts: Word-List Reading, Concept of Word (if needed), and Story Reading. The results of the word-list reading task are used to make a decision about the next step in the assessment. You will either do the Concept of Word assessment or skip that and go on to Story Reading. The results of the word identification assessment will

FIGURE 3.2. Sample spelling test that has been scored.

Child __Jill__   Date __8/10/97__

Sample map	First Sound	Final Sound	Vowel Sound	Blends and Digraphs	Silent Vowel Marker	Correct Spelling	Total Points
1 VN	✔	✔				van	2
2 PAT	✔	✔	✔			pet	3
3 RG	✔	✔				rug	2
4 saD	✔	✔	✔			sad ✔	4
5 poM	✔	✔	✔			plum	3
6 jP	✔	✔				chip	2
7 ShiN	✔	✔	✔	✔		shine	4
8 sct	✔	✔		✔		skate	3
9 floT	✔	✔	✔	✔		float	4
10 jret	✔	✔	✔	✔		treat	4

also give you a rough estimate of your child's reading level as shown in Figure 3.5 on page 42.

Word-List Reading

The first part of the word identification portion of the assessment is to ask students to read from the word lists. Make a copy of Form D.3 (on page 55), where the words are listed, or have the child read from the book, while you record his or her efforts on Form C.2, Word Identification in Lists (page 50). Cover all but one list at a time to focus the child's attention and reduce anxiety. Begin with the preprimer list. Say the following:

> "Here is a list of words. Put your finger on the first word. I want you to read each word you know. If you do not know a word, skip it and go to the next one. Some of these words will be difficult, so don't worry if you do not know every word."

Allow 3 or 4 seconds for each word and ask children to move on to the next one if they seem to stall. Children who can read 10 or more of the words on the preprimer list should be asked to read the primer list. Similarly, children who can read 10 of the words on the primer list should read from the first-grade list. Record responses on Form C.2, checking those that are known and writing in incorrect responses. If a child corrects herself immediately, put a check beside the word and give credit for that response. If the child offers no attempt, write NA or make a dash (—) beside the word. Record the total number of words read correctly at the bottom of each column and on Form B (page 47).

FIGURE 3.3. Spelling error analysis score sheet.

<u>Spelling Analysis Score Sheet</u>

These spellings will help you decide how to assign points to the spelling efforts your child makes. There are other possibilities, but these should guide your scoring in most cases. Some spelling substitutions (such as cd for sad) are logical and therefore deserve points. Remember, the main thing you are looking for here is the child's awareness of sounds in words, so a point is awarded for each sound that is represented logically. Points are also awarded for a silent vowel marker that accompanies a long vowel (such as the <u>a</u> in float or the <u>a</u> in treat). An extra point is awarded if a word is spelled correctly.

Word	First Sound	Final Sound	Vowel Sound	Blends & Digraphs	Silent Vowel Marker
van	v f <u>v</u>n	v<u>n</u> f<u>n</u>	<u>van</u> ven vin		
pet	p b <u>p</u>t <u>p</u>d <u>pet</u>	p<u>t</u> b<u>t</u>	<u>pet</u> pat pait bat		
rug	r w y <u>r</u>g <u>rug</u>	r<u>g</u> r<u>k</u> w<u>g</u> y<u>g</u> w<u>k</u>	<u>rug</u> rog rok roug wug		
sad	s c <u>sad</u>	s<u>d</u> c<u>d</u> s<u>t</u> c<u>t</u>	<u>sad</u> sid sed cad cid cet		
plum	p b <u>p</u>um <u>pl</u>m	p<u>m</u> b<u>m</u>	pl<u>u</u>m p<u>u</u>m p<u>ou</u>m p<u>o</u>lm	<u>plum</u> <u>pl</u>om <u>p</u>olm <u>pul</u>m	
chip	c h s j<u>p</u> <u>g</u>ip <u>chp</u>	c<u>p</u> ch<u>p</u> je<u>p</u> g<u>p</u> h<u>p</u> sh<u>p</u> si<u>p</u>	ch<u>i</u>p ch<u>e</u>p c<u>e</u>p c<u>i</u>p h<u>i</u>p j<u>i</u>p	<u>chip</u> <u>ch</u>ep	
shine	s h c <u>sh</u>in	s<u>n</u> sh<u>n</u> c<u>n</u> ch<u>n</u> ci<u>n</u> h<u>n</u>	sh<u>i</u>n sh<u>i</u>n ch<u>i</u>n h<u>a</u>n sh<u>a</u>n sh<u>y</u>n	<u>shin</u> <u>shin</u>e	s<u>i</u>ne sh<u>i</u>ne sh<u>i</u>en sh<u>y</u>ne
skate	s c <u>s</u>t <u>st</u>a <u>sk</u>t <u>c</u>t	s<u>t</u> c<u>t</u> s<u>g</u> cs<u>t</u> sg<u>t</u>	s<u>a</u>t sk<u>a</u>t sc<u>a</u>t sk<u>ay</u> sk<u>ae</u>t	<u>skat</u> <u>skate</u> <u>scate</u> <u>scat</u>	sk<u>a</u>te sk<u>ai</u>t sc<u>a</u>te sk<u>ae</u>t sk<u>ay</u>t
float	f v <u>f</u>t <u>f</u>ot <u>v</u>t	f<u>t</u> v<u>t</u> f<u>d</u> v<u>d</u> fo<u>t</u>	f<u>o</u>t fl<u>o</u>t f<u>ow</u>t fl<u>oa</u>t	<u>fl</u>ot <u>fl</u>oat <u>fl</u>ote <u>ful</u>ot	flo<u>a</u>te flo<u>a</u>t f<u>ow</u>t
treat	t g j ch <u>tr</u>t <u>te</u>t h	t<u>t</u> g<u>t</u> j<u>t</u> ch<u>t</u> tre<u>t</u> he<u>t</u>	t<u>e</u>t tr<u>ee</u> tr<u>e</u>t jr<u>e</u>t j<u>e</u>t gr<u>e</u>t	<u>tr</u>eet <u>tr</u>eat <u>tr</u>ee	tre<u>a</u>te tre<u>a</u>t tr<u>ee</u>t t<u>ee</u>t

Story Reading or Concept of Word?

If children could not name any words or only knew a few, go to the Concept of Word assessment described below and use the story *Sandcastle*. If children know five or more words, they probably have a concept of word. You can skip *Sandcastle* and start with *Sam*. If they read *Sam*, fulfilling the criterion described below, go on to *My Huge Dog Max*. For each story, there are specific directions on the recording sheets. Use the chart below to determine which stories to use and what the criterion of success is for each one. We have not included a primer-level story in this assessment. If children can successfully read *Sam* and *My Huge Dog Max*, then select a level 11 or 12 book from the leveled list of books in Appendix B and ask them to read it to you. Keep a tally of errors and calculate a percentage (number of errors/number of words in the story). Similarly, you can try books at levels 15 or 16 to test story reading at the first-grade level. You might also use an alternative assessment, such as a published Informal Reading Inventory (for instance, Leslie & Caldwell, 1995) if a child is reading above the preprimer level.

Score on preprimer list	Story to read	Criterion for success	Story to try next
0–4 words	*Sandcastle*	10 points	*Sam*
5–18	*Sam*	At least 25 words	*My Huge Dog Max*
19–20	*My Huge Dog Max*	At least 65 words	Primer level
	Primer story	90% accurate	First-grade level

Concept of Word Assessment with *Sandcastle*

To assess emergent readers' concept of word, you will need a copy of the story *Sandcastle* made into a little book (Form D.4) and Form B. Read each sentence to them as you point to the words. Next, they read along with you as you point again; finally, you ask them to read and point alone. After each sentence has been read, you will point to two designated words to be named. Follow the steps below and record children's responses on Form B after each sentence is completed.

Directions for Concept of Word Task

1. Explain to your child that you are going to read a story together.

2. Introduce the story by reading the title of the book and then discuss the first picture.

3. Read the sentence under the picture as you touch each word.

4. Ask the child to read *with you* as you point again.

5. Ask the child to read and point by herself. Score the pointing (2 points for accurate pointing, 0 if she makes a mistake).

6. Point to the underlined words as shown on the record sheet. Say "What is this word?" Record one point for each word identified correctly.

7. Repeat for each sentence.

Total the pointing scores and the word identification scores. If children are able to point accurately and can identify some of the words for a total score of 10 points or more, you should give them a chance to read the story *Sam*, as described below.

Word Identification in Story Reading

For word identification in story reading, you will need to have a copy of Forms C.3 and C.4 as well as the illustrated versions on pages 58 and 59 for the child to read. Directions for introducing the story and scoring it are included on the forms where you will record children's errors and scores. You can just use the illustrated versions on pages 58 and 59, or you can copy them, cut the pages apart, and staple them into the form of a little book. (Do *not* give the little book to the child or use it for instruction because you will need to use it for final assessment.)

Recording and Scoring Errors on the Story-Reading Task. If children get stuck on a word for more than 5 seconds or appeal to you for help, you can supply the word, but it will count as an error. Circle any words you supply. Cross out any words children misname on the record sheet and write above the word what your child said. Circle any words that are omitted and write in any added words. Indicate self-corrections by putting a check over the word, and do not count it as an error. Figure 3.4 illustrates some examples of reading errors children might make and how to mark them.

After the story has been read, you need to determine the number of words the child has read correctly by subtracting the number of errors from the total number of words in the story. Transfer the number of correctly read words to Form B (page 48) and compare them to the criteria for success. If a child is able to read accurately 25 of the 30 words in the story Sam, try the story *My Huge Dog Max*. If a child is able to read 62 of the words in *My Huge Dog Max*, try a primer-level story. Sometimes, you will find that a child just cannot read the story. If you are having to supply every word or two, just stop the testing there. Say "Let's read this together" and proceed to read the rest of it in a choral fashion.

FIGURE 3.4. Samples of reading errors and how to mark them.

1. Sam ~~has~~ a big dog.   ("had" was substituted for "has")
   (had written above "has")

2. Sam has a (big) dog.   ("big" was omitted or supplied by the tester)

3. Sam has a˅ big dog.   ("very" was added)
   (very written above the caret)

4. Sam ~~has~~ a big dog.   ("had" was corrected to "has")
   (had ✓ written above "has")

The Assessment Summary Sheet

Transfer scores from Form B recording sheets to the Assessment Summary Sheet (Form A, page 45) and staple or clip all the other testing materials together. Keep the results of the initial assessment in a secure place. You will be referring to these test results to decide on the best lesson plan to use for your child, to help you select appropriate reading materials, and to plan specific instructional activities as described in Chapters 4 and 5. You will find that the numerical scores on the summary sheet offer a useful comparison to assess progress when you are ready to determine the effectiveness of the tutoring program and your work with a particular child.

Interpreting the Results of the Assessment

Using the Results to Determine Which Lesson Plan to Use

This book describes lesson plans for readers who are at either the emergent stage (Chapter 4) or the early reader stage (Chapter 5). The results of the initial assessment will help you decide which plan to use, although it is certainly possible that some children will fall between, and you will need to draw on ideas from both plans. Begin by comparing the assessment results with the types of readers described below:

- *Emergent readers* may still lack complete alphabet knowledge, may not have much awareness of sounds in words, and may not be able to point accurately to the words in a sentence (Concept of Word). In terms of word identification, the emergent reader may not know any words on the preprimer list, or may know less than half of them (< 10 words). Your child's ability to read *Sandcastle*, *Sam*, or *My Huge Dog Max* will determine the levels of reading materials they will be using, as described in the next section.

- *Early readers* know their alphabet, can spell many of the sounds in a word, and can also read most of the words in the preprimer list (15 or more) and some of the primer list. Early readers should be able to read *Sam* and *My Huge Dog Max* according to the criterion for success.

Determining the Child's Reading Level in Order to Select Appropriate Books

The chart in Figure 3.5 can serve as a starting point for deciding which level books to use with your child. Exact placements will depend upon how well the child actually reads at that level and can only be determined by observing how well the child does on several books at that level.

Emergent Readers in Book Levels 1–3

If children cannot point accurately to the words in *Sandcastle*, they may not even know what a word is and may have great difficulty finding where words begin and end on the page. The simple books from the first three levels are writ-

FIGURE 3.5.   Criteria for selecting books.

Criteria for Selecting Books at a Range of Levels			
Child Can Read	*Word-List Reading*	*Book-Level Range*	*Type of Reader*
Sandcastle	Few, if any, (0–4) on preprimer list	1–3 (Readiness)	Emergent (1)
Sam	Some (5–9 words) on preprimer list	3–7 (Preprimer 1 and 2)	Emergent (2)
My Huge Dog Max	>50% (10–16 words) on preprimer list	7–9 (Preprimer 3)	Emergent (3)
Primer story at @ 90% accuracy	80–100% (16–20 words) on preprimer list >50% on primer list	9–12 (Primer)	Early (Primer)
First-grade story at @ 90% accuracy	80–90% on primer list	13–16 (First grade)	Early (First grade)
Early Second-grade story @ 92%	90–100% on primer list @ 75% on First grade	17–20 (Early Second grade)	Second grade

ten with only a few words per page, which will enable these children to match the words they say with the words on the page by pointing as they read. These books are also quite predictable; the words repeat in patterns and are cued by the pictures, and they sometimes rhyme (for example, the sentence pattern "I see a tiger" changes to "I see a zebra" on the next page, and the pictures cue the respective animal names). Even if children can point accurately to the words in *Sandcastle*, they may not have been able to read *Sam* to criterion. In this case, it is unlikely that they know many words, and they still need to be in the easiest levels. Observations during tutoring will help you determine whether to start with book levels 1, 2, or 3. If children can name and point to the words accurately after several readings, they are probably at the right level. They should also be able to use the picture cues and the beginning sound of words to help name words. If not, they may need to be moved back to an easier level.

Emergent Readers in Book Levels 3–7

If children *can* read *Sam* to criterion and know *some* words on the preprimer word list, they are probably ready to begin reading the preprimer materials in book levels 3–7. These stories have a limited range of words in repeated sentence patterns, with two or three sentences on a page. The pictures will continue to help children identify many of the words. Again, observations during tutoring will determine which books within this range make a comfortable fit. If children have no trouble at all on the first or second reading, they may be ready for a higher level. On the other hand, if they are still making some mistakes by the third rereading, they may need to move back to an easier level.

Emergent Readers in Book Levels 7–9

If children can read *My Huge Dog Max* and know about half of the words on the preprimer list, they are ready to try books in levels 7–9. Although these books will still have only two or three sentences per page, the sentence patterns will vary, and there will be a wider range of words in a story.

Early Readers at Book Levels 9–16

Children who can read at the primer level or first-grade level with 90% accuracy or better are ready for books at levels 9–16. These books may still have some repetition of sentence patterns and many illustrations, but the sentences are longer, and there will be many different words in a story. Children will be doing less rereading of these books and should be able to read them the first time through with at least 90% accuracy. That means no more than one error in 10 words.

Readers at Second-Grade Level and Above

If children are in third grade or higher, yet reading at an early second-grade level, they will still benefit from individual tutoring and the activities described in Chapter 5. They can be placed in reading materials at levels 16–20 and above. Observe how accurately children are able to read books at a particular level, and be sure that they can read 90% of the words at a smooth and steady pace. If they can read just about every word correctly and quickly, try a book at a higher level. If they read with more than one error in 10 words and read slowly and hesitantly try books at an easier level.

Using the Alphabet, Picture Sorting, and Spelling to Plan Word Study

Alphabet Assessment

If a child knows about 20 lowercase letters (out of 26), then work on the alphabet can be addressed incidentally during reading and writing activities. For example, the child might be asked to find words that contain a targeted letter or point to a letter in the title of a book. On the other hand, if a child knows less than half his letters, he will benefit from some intensive, systematic work on letters both while reading and writing and during game-like activities. Make a note of any letters that the child reverses during assessment and include work on those.

Sound-Sorting Assessment

If your child cannot sort the picture cards perfectly, you will definitely need to begin your phonics instruction with initial consonant sounds.

FIGURE 3.6. Using spelling to determine phonics.

Using Spellings to Determine Phonics Instruction		
Spelling Sample Errors	What the Child Knows	What to Work on
van = RT, pet = ML	Words are made of letters but not matched to sounds.	1. Alphabet, if needed. 2. Picture sorts of beginning sounds.
van = F, pet = PD, rug = G	Some consonant sounds are represented but incomplete.	1. Alphabet, if needed. 2. Picture sorts of beginning sounds.
van = VN, pet = PT, rug = RG, chip = JP, plum = PM, float = FOT	Single beginning and final consonants correct for the most part. Few, if any, vowels in middle.	1. Compare same-vowel word families. 2. Picture sorts of digraphs and blends.
rug = ROG, pet = PAT, plum = POLM, chip = CHEP, shine = CHIN	Single beginning and final consonants correct. Blends and digraphs may still be confused. Short vowels are used but confused.	1. Compare mixed-vowel word families. 2. Compare short vowels in nonrhyming words. 3. Include words with blends and digraphs.
plum = PLUM, chip = CHIP, float = FLOTE, shine = SHIN, treat = TREET	Short vowels are correct for the most part, and blends and digraphs are largely correct. Long vowels are spelled with correct long vowel sound but incorrect silent vowel marker.	1. Compare long and short vowel sounds. 2. Compare long vowels spelled with different patterns.

Spelling Assessment

Children's spelling efforts give us an insight into their ability to separate the sounds in a word and match those sounds to letters. Figure 3.6 will assist you in interpreting spelling as a key to the phonics instruction children will need.

Assessment Recording Forms

In the pages that follow, you will find all the forms you need to complete the assessment of alphabet, letter–sound knowledge, and word-list reading. You will also find the stories *Sandcastle, Sam, My Huge Dog Max,* and their accompanying record forms. If your child can read stories at a higher level than these, you will need to select a book at a primer level, as suggested earlier, or use a published Informal Reading Inventory (IRI), such as the one by Leslie & Caldwell (1995), which can provide accurate diagnostic information. Brief directions are repeated for most of the assessment tasks, but be sure you are familiar with the complete directions in this chapter as well.

FORM A. **Assessment Summary Sheet for Emergent and Early Readers**

Child _____ Date of Birth _____

Examiner _____ Teacher/Grade _____

		Test Date 1 __/__/__	Test Date 2 __/__/__	Test Date 3 __/__/__
Alphabet Knowledge				
Capital Letters	(26)	_____	_____	_____
Lowercase Letters	(26)	_____	_____	_____
Letter Production	(26)	_____	_____	_____
Total Score	(78)	_____	_____	_____
Lettersound Knowledge				
Picture Sorting	(12)	_____	_____	_____
Spelling	(50)	_____	_____	_____
Total Score	(62)	_____	_____	_____
Word Identification in Lists				
Preprimer	(20)	_____	_____	_____
Primer	(20)	_____	_____	_____
First Grade	(20)	_____	_____	_____
Total Score	(60)	_____	_____	_____
Concept of Word (in *Sandcastle*)				
Pointing	(8)	_____	_____	_____
Word Identification	(8)	_____	_____	_____
Total Score	(16)	_____	_____	_____
Word Identification in Stories				
PP 2 *Sam*	(30 words)	_____	_____	_____
PP 3 *My Huge Dog Max*	(72)	_____	_____	_____
Primer		_____	_____	_____
First Grade		_____	_____	_____

Observations during Testing

FORM B. Assessment Recording Forms

Child _____ Examiner _____ Date _____

Alphabet Knowledge

1. Letter Identification (26 possible for each case)

Directions: Ask the students to name the letters on page 53. Record responses here. Circle any incorrect responses. Reversals are incorrect. Self-corrections are counted correct if they are immediate.

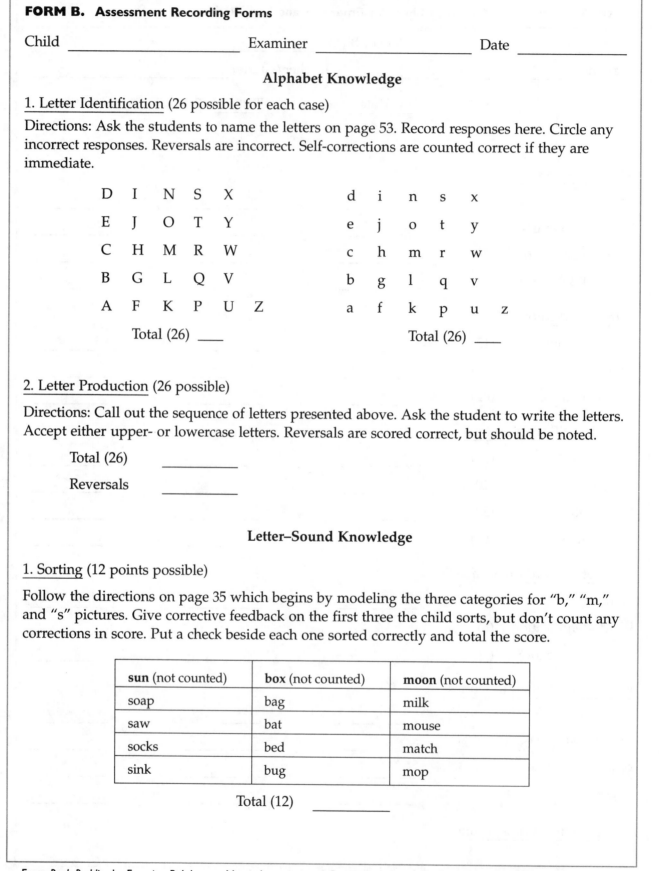

D	I	N	S	X		d	i	n	s	x
E	J	O	T	Y		e	j	o	t	y
C	H	M	R	W		c	h	m	r	w
B	G	L	Q	V		b	g	l	q	v
A	F	K	P	U	Z	a	f	k	p	u	z

Total (26) ____   Total (26) ____

2. Letter Production (26 possible)

Directions: Call out the sequence of letters presented above. Ask the student to write the letters. Accept either upper- or lowercase letters. Reversals are scored correct, but should be noted.

Total (26)   _____

Reversals   _____

Letter–Sound Knowledge

1. Sorting (12 points possible)

Follow the directions on page 35 which begins by modeling the three categories for "b," "m," and "s" pictures. Give corrective feedback on the first three the child sorts, but don't count any corrections in score. Put a check beside each one sorted correctly and total the score.

sun (not counted)	**box** (not counted)	**moon** (not counted)
soap	bag	milk
saw	bat	mouse
socks	bed	match
sink	bug	mop

Total (12)   _____

FORM B. Assessment Recording Forms (continued)

2. Spelling (50 possible points)

Directions: Make a copy of Form C.1 and fold on dotted line. Begin by modeling the word "map" in the unnumbered box as described on page 36. Do *not* elongate the sounds for any other words. Refer to page 38 for help on scoring.

(map)   1. van   3. rug   5. plum   7. shine   9. float

         2. pet   4. sad   6. chip   8. skate   10. treat

Total (possible total = 50) _____

Word Identification

1. Word Identification in Lists

Directions: Record responses in the boxes on Form C.2 while the child reads from the list on page 36. Begin with the preprimer list. If the student correctly identifies 10 words or more on the preprimer list, continue with the primer list. If the student correctly identifies 10 words or more on the primer list, continue with the first-grade list.

Preprimer   (possible total = 20)   _____

Primer   (possible total = 20)   _____

First Grade   (possible total = 20)   _____

2. Concept of Word with *Sandcastle* (16 points possible) (For children who know fewer than five words on the preprimer list).

Directions:

   (1) Introduce the story, *Sandcastle*, by reading the title and then discussing the picture on the first page. Say "This is Alvin. What is Alvin doing?"

   (2) Read the first sentence pointing to each word. "Down here it says 'Alvin is playing in the sand.'"

   (3) Ask the child to read along with you as you repeat the sentence and point to each word. Say "Read this with me."

   (4) Ask the child to read the sentence alone and point to each word. Say "Now it is your turn to read the sentence." Point to each word as you read.

   (5) Point to each of the two words in the sentence as indicated on the next page and say "What is this word?" (For example, point to "sand" and then to "playing" in the first sentence).

   (6) Repeat for each page. Begin by briefly discussing the picture and then read the sentence before asking the child to read along and then independently. Test the two individual words before going to the next page.

FORM B. Assessment Recording Forms (continued)

<u>Scoring Pointing:</u> Give 2 points for each sentence pointed to correctly. Also give 2 points if the child corrects himself without prompting. Give zero points for each sentence *not* pointed to correctly.

<u>Scoring Word Identification:</u> Give 1 point for each word correctly identified (there are two in each sentence).

<u>Sentence</u>	<u>Pointing</u>	<u>Word Identification</u>	
1. Alvin is <u>playing</u> in the <u>sand</u>. 2 1	_____ (2)	_____ , _____	(1 each)
2. <u>He</u> makes a <u>big</u> castle. 1 2	_____ (2)	_____ , _____	(1 each)
3. His little <u>brother</u> knocks <u>it</u> down. 2 1	_____ (2)	_____ , _____	(1 each)
4. Alvin <u>starts</u> all <u>over</u>. 1 2	_____ (2)	_____ , _____	(1 each)

Total Pointing (8 possible points)   _____

Total Word Identification (8 possible)   _____

Total Score for Concept of Word (16)   _____

3. Word Identification in Stories

Directions: If the child could read at least five of the preprimer words, begin with *Sam*. Continue with *My Huge Dog Max* if the child reads at least 25 words correctly in *Sam*. Introduce each book with the script attached to the examiner's copy. Do not choral or echo read. If the student pauses for more than 5 seconds, supply the word and ask the student to continue. Supplied words are counted as errors. Self-corrections are *not* counted as errors.

<u>Number of Words Read Correctly</u>

Preprimer 2 *Sam* (30 words)   _____   (criterion for success = 25)

Preprimer 3 *My Big Dog Max* (72 words)   _____   (criterion for success = 62)

Primer (calculate percent)   _____   (criterion for success = 90%)

FORM C.1. Spelling Assessment

Child_____   Date_____

Sample		First Sound	Final Sound	Vowel Sound	Blends and Digraphs	Silent Vowel Marker	Correct Spelling	Total Points
1							van	
2							pet	
3							rug	
4							sad	
5							plum	
6							chip	
7							shine	
8							skate	
9							float	
10							treat	

FORM C. 2. Word Identification in Lists

Child _____ Date _____

Check correct responses, write in substitutions, and check immediate self-corrections.

	Preprimer	Primer	First Grade
1.	the	girl	road
2.	at	yellow	boy
3.	can	mother	move
4.	with	swim	horse
5.	my	sheep	king
6.	go	old	once
7.	did	put	sometimes
8.	run	very	family
9.	red	green	never
10.	bus	eat	paper
11.	get	happy	try
12.	see	play	visit
13.	like	what	grandfather
14.	to	every	ago
15.	she	work	eggs
16.	box	farm	cloud
17.	and	bear	barn
18.	dog	rabbit	table
19.	is	toy	afternoon
20.	up	new	dear
	Total _____	Total _____	Total _____

Go on to the next list if the child can name 10 or more of the words in a list.

FORM C. 3. **Story-Reading Assessment Form for Sam**

Child _____ Date _____

<u>Directions for Introducing the Story</u>: Introduce the story with the following statements and questions. Do not read the story to the child.

    1. Read and point to the title of the story. "The name of this story is *Sam*."

    2. Look at the pictures on the first page and say "This must be Sam. What kind of a pet does he have? It looks like he has a big dog."

    3. Look at the pictures on the second page and say "The dog is looking at the cup. Can he get it? He is so big he can get the cup on the counter."

    4. Look at the pictures on the last page. "Oh no, up he went and down went the cup. What a mess! Let's see if you can read this story about Sam."

<u>Directions for Scoring:</u> If children pause for more than 5 seconds or appeal to you for help, give them the word but circle it below as an error. Cross out words that are misnamed and write above what the child says, circle omissions, and write in additions. If children correct themselves, put a check over the word and do not count it as an error.

Sam has a dog.

Sam has a big dog.

The dog is so big he can get the cup.

Look out Sam!

Up goes the dog.

Down goes the cup.

Words identified correctly in the story (30 words possible) _____

FORM C. 4.   **Story-Reading Assessment Form for *My Huge Dog Max***

Child _____   Date _____

<u>Directions for Introducing the Story:</u> Introduce the story with the following statements and questions. Do not read the story to the child.

1. Read and point to the words in the title of the story. Emphasize the word "huge" as you point to it.

2. Look at the picture on the first page and say "This must be Max. He sure does look huge. He is covered in black spots." Point to the word "spots."

3. Look at the picture on the second page and ask "What do you think he likes to do with Max? It looks like Max is excited about going out to play ball." Point to the word "ball." "He is wagging his tail." Point to "tail."

4. Look at the picture on the third page. Say "Max makes Sam happy when he's sad."

5. Look at the picture on the last page. Say "Where is Max now? Do you think Mom would like to see him there? Where would Mom want Max to be? Now you read this story about that huge dog Max."

I have a dog. His name is Max.

Max is a huge dog with black spots.

I like to play ball with Max.

When Max sees the ball he wags his tail.

He knows we will go out and play.

I love Max and he loves me.

Max can make me happy when I am sad.

I take good care of Max.

He sleeps under my bed.

That's what my Mom thinks.

Words identified correctly in the story (72 words possible) _____

FORM D.1. Alphabet Naming (child's copy)

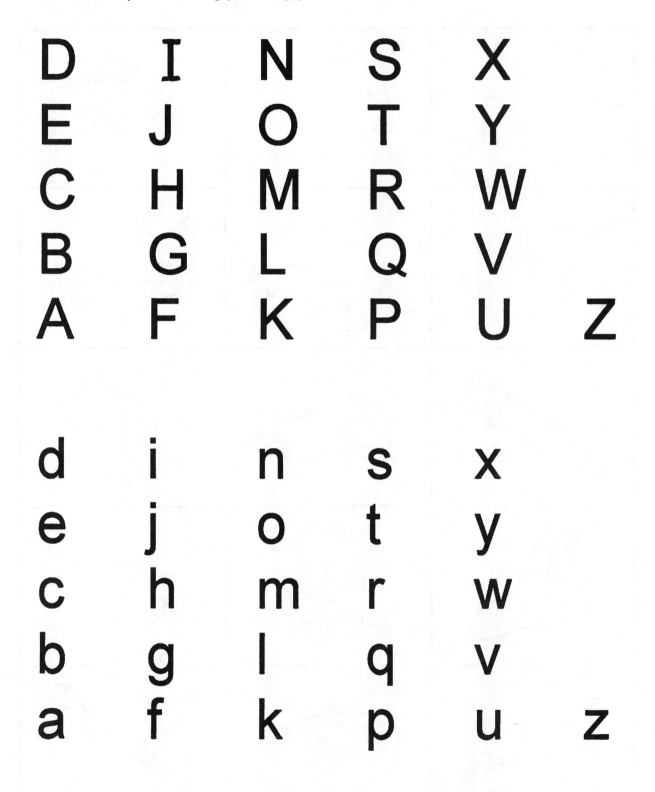

D	I	N	S	X	
E	J	O	T	Y	
C	H	M	R	W	
B	G	L	Q	V	
A	F	K	P	U	Z

d	i	n	s	x	
e	j	o	t	y	
c	h	m	r	w	
b	g	l	q	v	
a	f	k	p	u	z

FORM D.2. Pictures for Sound Awareness Sorting (cut apart for child to sort)

FORM D.3. Word Lists for Word Identification (list for child to read)

the	girl	road
at	yellow	boy
can	mother	move
with	swim	horse
my	sheep	king
go	old	once
did	put	sometimes
run	very	family
red	green	never
bus	eat	paper
get	happy	try
see	play	visit
like	what	grandfather
to	every	ago
she	work	eggs
box	farm	clouds
and	bear	barn
dog	rabbit	table
is	toy	afternoon
up	new	dear

FORM D.4. *Sandcastle* (copy for child to read)

Sand Castle

Alvin is playing in the sand.

He makes a big castle.

FORM D.4. *Sandcastle* (copy for child to read)

His little brother knocks it down.

Alvin starts all over.

FORM D.5. *Sam* (copy for child to read)

Sam

Sam has a dog.
Sam has a big dog.

The dog is so big
he can get the cup.

Look out Sam.
Up goes the dog.
Down goes the cup.

FORM D.6. *My Huge Dog Max* (copy for child to read)

My Huge Dog Max

I have a dog.
His name is Max.
Max is a huge dog with
black spots.

I like to play ball with Max.
When Max sees the ball
he wags his tail.
He knows we will go out
and play.

I love Max and he loves
me.
Max can make me happy
when I am sad.

I take good care of Max.
He sleeps under my bed.
That's what my Mom
thinks.

References

Leslie, L., & Caldwell, J. (1995). *The qualitative reading inventory,* 2nd ed. New York: Addison Wesley Longman.

Morris, D. (1992) What constitutes at-risk screening children for first grade reading intervention. *Best Practices in School Speech-Language Pathology, 2,* 43–51.

CHAPTER 4

General Tutoring Plan for the Emergent Reader

This chapter presents the lesson plan for the emergent reader. The next chapter presents the lesson tutoring plan for early readers. Be sure you have assessment information and have considered the criteria in Chapter 3 to determine whether your child is an emergent reader or an early reader. Below is a brief description of the four components of the lesson plan. The rest of the chapter describes each part in detail. This chapter is addressed to the tutor, and we use "you" and "your child" throughout.

Overview of the Emergent Reader Plan

The lesson plan for the emergent reader consists of four parts:

1. *Rereading familiar materials* (10–15 minutes). During this warm-up and practice, children reread books they have read in previous sessions.

2. *Word study and phonics* (10–12 minutes). In this part, tutors and children look for words in stories that are known. Tutors write the words on cards to form a word bank and later use these and other word cards for phonics instruction.

3. *Writing for sounds* (5–10 minutes). In this part, tutors dictate one or two sentences for their children to spell as best they can.

4. *Reading new materials* (10–15 minutes). In the last part of the plan, tutors introduce a new book. The tutors read the title of the book and talk with their children about the pictures and story before the children read it for themselves.

A sample lesson plan is reproduced in Figure 4.1, and a blank form for emergent lesson plans can be found in Appendix A. As you work through each part of the plan, write in comments to describe how well your child accomplished the various tasks. These comments will serve as guides for future planning and provide important documentation of your child's progress. The questions at the end of each section give you ideas about the kinds of things to write in the comments section of the plan. There are also questions to assess your own developing skills as a tutor.

Emergent Reader Lesson Plan
Part I: Rereading Familiar Material

Every tutoring session opens with the reading of three or more familiar books, including the new book introduced in the previous lesson. This part of the lesson should last 10 to 15 minutes. Rereading gives students the chance to develop smooth, accurate reading in easy, familiar materials. Children see the same words over and over again, and increase the number of words they recognize automatically. This rereading also serves as a warm-up and confidence builder. As children read with confidence, they are more likely to read with understanding and enjoyment. Books are retired from the warm-up routine after four to six rereadings. Children then move on to other books that they have not yet learned to read smoothly and accurately.

Getting Started with Rereading

In the very first tutoring session, you won't have any familiar books to reread, so you will begin with one or two book introductions (see Part IV of the lesson plan described later in this chapter). Gradually, you will build up a collection of books that have been read before, and you will use these for the rereading. When the child has read a book four to six times, it is retired from the collection. You may also retire a book if it is too hard, too easy, or if the child simply doesn't like it.

When getting started, avoid asking your child "Would you like to read?" They may answer "No!" and then where would you be? Instead, announce that it is time to read, and offer your child a choice from a collection of four or five books that have been read before. You might start by rereading the story that was introduced at the end of the last session and then go on to reread four or five additional books. Encourage your child to point to the words as she reads, especially if she gets off track, and be prepared to provide help as needed. Read how Stanley and Malcolm work together on the first part of the plan.

Stanley: Malcolm, let's get to work. Here's the new book we read last week. *(Malcolm rereads new book from last session stumbling over only one word.)* Good job. I like the way you went back and figured out that word you didn't know. Here are the other books you've read. Which one do you want to read next? *(Malcolm selects a book and reads the sentence "I saw a lion at the zoo" as "I saw a tiger at the zoo." He doesn't pause, but after he reads the rest of the book,*

FIGURE 4.1. Sample lesson plan, full size.

Emergent Plan Student Malcolm **Tutor** Stanley **Date** Oct 12 **Lesson #** 8

Lesson Plan	Description of Planned Activities	Time	Outcomes and Comments
Rereading	Materials: Big Wheels / At the Zoo / Sandy / Rhyme Book	10	Problems? Great job on Sandy! "Big Wheels" confused "agin" for "lion"; has need the first lttr. Getting tired of rhyme - Send home next time.
Word Study	1. Word Bank: Look for words in Sandy. Review old words	12	Picked five new words. Called rabbit ram. Played picking with words he missed and got them all.
	2. Picture/Word Sort: Sort J K L Pictures		Sorted J, K, L pictures easily. Add another sound?
	3. Writing Sort: Spell two words to each letter. Let him pile pictures		Spelled lamp LP, keg KE, and jar JR - no vowels.
	4. Push It Say It: L, J, ET Make jet and let		Doing better on blending!
Writing	Sentence: ~~Jump in the lake.~~ I saw a lion at the zoo.	8	Child's Effort: I s a lin at the zoo. Added the i in lion after saying it slowly. The remembered how to spell at and zoo!
New Reading	Book: My Pizza Level: 4 Introduction notes: Read title, talk about the toppings and point to words. Use pattern: Put on the.....	8	Problems? Called pepperoni sausage but corrected himself using P. Couldn't remember "oven". Talk about it before reading next time. 2nd & 3rd nothing went well - he lines it. Read Book 3 Times

Good session! Remember to come 15 minutes earlier next week.

> *Stanley revisits the error.)* Let's go back to this page for a minute. Look at this word *(points to "lion")* Can that word be tiger? How does tiger start?
>
> Malcolm: Tiger starts with a "t."
>
> Stanley: Right. A tiger is a big cat like the one in the picture but tigers have stripes. What big cat can start with an "l"? What word could that be?
>
> Malcolm: Lion?
>
> Stanley: Read that sentence again and see if "lion" will work. *(Malcolm rereads the sentence correctly.)* That works. You figured out that word. Now pick another book to read.

Continue in this vein until all of the books in the rereading collection have been read. Keep a list of all the books your student reads. (A "Books I Have Read" form for this purpose is included in Appendix A). Each time a story or poem is read, place a tally mark beside it. For beginners, it is a reasonable goal to expect them to read each book between four to six times. Sometimes, students are more willing to do rereading when they have a set goal to attain and can see their progress in the tally marks. You might even let them make the tallies.

Questions You Might Have

What Do I Do When My Child Has Trouble Reading?

During rereading time, your student should be zipping through one thing after another with very few errors or hesitations. However, he will forget words he knew the session before and confuse words with one another. If he hesitates or makes an error, the first thing you do is *nothing*! Resist the impulse to correct it immediately. Give him the chance to work it out or discover the error for himself. That may not happen until he gets to the end of the sentence and realizes that something didn't make sense.

Beginners often remember words, not as entire letter strings, but in bits and pieces. What they remember about "car" may be only that it starts with "c." In that case, they may well confuse it with "cat" and read "I saw a *cat*" instead of "I saw a *car*." Listen to the words your student substitutes and consider what parts, if any, of that word fit what is on the page. Help the child to see the source of the problem when appropriate. In the previous example, Malcolm used the picture as a clue and came up with "tiger" instead of "lion." Both words made sense, but he probably was not using any letters as cues. Stanley asked Malcolm to take another look at the word and helped him use letter sounds as a clue.

When your child makes an error, wait and see if she corrects it herself. If she doesn't, draw the child's attention to it gently by saying something like

> "Did that make sense to you? Let's try it again."
>
> "Oops, I think you left out a word. Point to each word as you read that sentence again."
>
> "That was a good try, but let's look at this word again."
>
> "What else could that word be?"

Often, your child will come to a word she doesn't know and simply stop or appeal to you for help. Tutors are often tempted to say "Sound it out" as a strategy, but emergent readers cannot yet sound their way through an unfamiliar word because they know very little about vowel sounds. However, they may be able to use the first sound, which is often a consonant, to make a sensible guess. You might use the following prompt "Try that sentence again and when you come to this word (*point to the problem word*) say the first sound."

When your child gets stuck on a word, there is often no better response than just to give her the word, especially if it is near the beginning of a sentence. You might want to make a copy of the prompts on page 97 for ideas about appropriate ways to intervene. Keep them handy for reference until you become good at using them. However, if your child is having too much trouble, she needs to be reading books at an easier level. Missing more than two or three words in a book after several rereadings is usually a sign that the book is too hard. Take a step back, and try books at an easier level.

What If My Child Just Seems to Be Memorizing the Book?

The emergent reader *does* rely upon memory and illustrations a great deal, and this is a good thing. Without these sources of support, emergent readers would not be able to read much at all. But even when we ask children to point to the words as they read (and they should), they may not be paying close attention to the words themselves, and if children are not paying attention to the words, they won't learn them. Since children rely on the pictures as clues when they read, you can try covering up the pictures as a way to see if they are really using the print. Another way to "glue children to print" is to have them read from a computer-generated or a typed-text-only copy of a familiar story printed on a single sheet of paper without illustrations. This text-only copy is particularly appropriate for favorite books that have been read a number of times. These typed or printed copies can be used as additional material during the rereading routine, and can be stapled together into personal readers for children to take home.

**Observation Guide for the
Rereading Part of the Lesson Plan**

Ask yourself the following questions to assess how well your child did. Record your observations on the lesson plan as a guide for future planning.

- Did the child read with interest? What did he or she particularly enjoy?
- Which books were read easily, and are any ready to be retired?
- Which books posed problems, and what were those problems?
- How did you and the child work out any problems?
- How much time was spent rereading?
- What will you do differently next time?

Emergent Reader Lesson Plan
Part II: Word Study

The second part of the lesson plan is called word study. Word study helps children learn new words, teaches letter–sound correspondences, improves children's skills in figuring out unfamiliar words when they read, and helps them learn to spell words. Word study consists of two parts: (1) word-bank work, and (2) phonics instruction. Altogether, this part of the lesson should take about 10 to 12 minutes.

1. *Word bank:* The first step in the word study part of the lesson plan involves adding to and reviewing word-bank words. A word bank is a collection of words, written on small, individual cards or slips of paper, that a child knows well enough to recognize in isolation. The word bank serves three important purposes. (1) In the process of collecting and reviewing word-bank words, children match the words they say with the printed words in the text. This is particularly helpful for those children who lack a concept of word and are unsure of where words begin and end on the page. (2) As children review their word-bank cards, they must pay close attention to the print. This increases the familiarity of the words, and children build a collection of words that can be recognized immediately, without effort. These words are often called *sight words,* because they can be read instantly, "at first sight." (3) Word-bank words provide a collection of familiar words for phonics instruction.

2. *Phonics instruction:* In the earliest stage, phonics instruction helps children learn the one-to-one connections between sounds and letters (such as the fact that the words "bell," "bat," and "bug" all begin with the letter "b"). Later, they will learn about familiar chunks or patterns of letters (such as the fact that the letters AT in c*at,* m*at* and r*at*tle always sound the same). Instructional activities consist of sorting tasks, first with picture cards, then with word-bank cards, as the child's collection of known words grows. Each of these components is described in more detail below.

Word Bank

A word bank is a child's personal collection of known words written on small cards (it is better if you write the words neatly rather than have the child write them) and kept in an envelope or plastic baggy to be reviewed, sorted, and played with regularly, as described below. Word-bank words are intended to be *known* words, that is, words that are recognized immediately by the child. Children should *not* be expected to sound out word-bank words during review. If a word is unknown, there are several other ways to help the child, as Stanley does below:

> Stanley: You read those books really well today. Let's go back to *Sandy* and see if there are any words you would like to add to your word bank today. *(Stanley lays* Sandy *on the table and Malcolm turns through the pages.)* Tell me some words that you know.
>
> Malcolm: *(pointing to the word "ran")* This word is "ran."
>
> Stanley: You are right. I am going to write that on a card for you. Find a few more. *(Malcom pages through the book and picks out "me," "fast," "you," and "rabbit" while Stanley writes them on cards.)* Now let's see if you remember these words. *(He hands the word cards to Malcolm, and Malcolm reads each one.)* Malcolm, we have five new words to add to the word bank today.

At the next tutoring session, Stanley leads Malcolm through a review of all the words in the word bank:

> Stanley: Let's see if you can read all the words in your word bank. *(Malcolm goes through his word cards. When he comes to "rabbit" he calls it "run.")* Well, Malcolm, that word starts with an "r" just like "run" but look at it again. *(Malcolm can't come up with any other answer.)* Let's look back in your book where you saw that word before. *(Stanley opens* Sandy *to the page where the word appears.)* Do you see it here? What is that word?
>
> Malcolm: *(pointing to the word)* Rabbit! That word is "rabbit."
>
> Stanley: That's it. We'll put "rabbit" in our "practice pile" and come back to it later. *(Several other words end up in the "practice pile" for review, and after reading all the known words, Stanley lays out all of the unknown words face up.)* Let's play "pick up." I'm going to call out these words and you find them for me. Where is "rabbit"? *(Malcolm picks it out easily.)* Great! How did you know that word was "rabbit"?
>
> Malcolm: It starts with an "r" and it has two "b's" in it.

Creating the Word Bank

From the very first tutoring session, you should begin to create a word bank, even if your child hasn't read anything yet. The first words might include the child's name, your name, family members' names, a friend's name, and so on. You might simply ask your student if there are any words that she knows or would like to learn. Common words such as "I," "the," and "a" may be known. After a few sessions, you can begin to collect words from the materials that you are rereading during the first part of the lesson plan.

In the Charlottesville Book Buddies tutorial, the little books used for reading have library pockets in the back with word cards. The words are selected because they are *high-frequency words* that children are likely to see in other stories (for example, "girl," "this," "with," "red") or words with a particular phonics feature (for example, "bee," "buzz," and "bus" all start with "b"), or interesting words (for example, "dinosaur," "skateboard," "lizard"). The tutor takes the word cards from the library pocket in the back of the book, spreads them out on the table, and asks the child to read the words she knows. New words that the child can easily identify are then copied onto the alphabetic word-bank list (in Appendix A) and onto cards to be added to the child's word bank. Two to 10 new words may be added each session.

If you don't have books with pockets of word cards already prepared, this routine can be slightly modified, as Stanley did with Malcolm. After the rereading, you or the child can just pick words in the story to name. Known words can be copied onto cards and added to the child's word bank. If you use text-only copies of stories, ask your child to underline words that he knows, and then those words can be added to his word bank.

Reviewing the Word Bank

The following activities provide a variety of ways to review the word bank collection:

1. *Simple sort:* Hand the collection of words to your child and ask him to go through and read each one, putting known words in one pile and unknown words in another (Malcolm's "practice pile"). These unknown words are good ones to include in the "pick-up" game described next.

2. *Pick-up:* Lay out 6–10 words on the table face up. Ask your child to find and pick up the word you name. Reverse roles. Let your child name the words and you pick them up. Up the ante for this review by laying out words that begin with the same letters, such as "big" and "boy" and "better." This requires that the student attend to more than just the first letter. This is a good time to put out those words that the child often confuses. Here are some variations for pick-up:

Variations for Pick-up Game	Pick up words that all begin with a certain letter (perhaps one you have been studying in the phonics part of the plan).
	Pick up words that all contain a certain letter (perhaps one the child often confuses).
	Pick up words that rhyme with . . .
	Pick up words that start like "f-f-f-ire."

3. *Bingo or lotto:* Prepare a board by lining off a plain sheet of paper into boxes, either a 3 × 3 array or 4 × 4 (large enough to write in words). Select enough words from the word bank to write in each box (see Figure 4.2). You

FIGURE 4.2. Word-bank bingo and sentences.

and your child can share the task of selecting the words and writing them. You will need something to cover the spaces as the words are called. Pennies, small squares of paper, poker chips, letter tiles, and so on will do the job. To play the game, shuffle the word cards and turn them face down. The caller draws a card, names it, and the player covers the word on the board. Three or four in a row is a winner. Switch roles and play again. To compete, keep track of how many plays it takes to win.

4. *Create sentences:* Once your child has a good-sized collection of word cards, you can create sentences. Begin by making a sentence yourself, then ask your child to read it. Or call out a sentence for your child to make with the available words. You might want to lay out a limited collection of words to choose from. For example, lay out "like," "my," "I," and "dog," and ask your child to make the sentence "I like my dog." Eventually, you want your child to make up his or her own sentences, but continue to make it a joint effort if needed.

5. *Rebuild words:* Select a word from the word bank and have your child spell it with letter cards (see Appendix A for letter cards you can cut apart), link letters (commercial, puzzle-like letters), or magnetic letters. You can also simply write the word on another word card and cut it apart to put back in order. You might call out the easiest words (three- and four-letter words such as "was" or "here") to be spelled on paper or on a chalkboard. Let your child check and correct his spelling by looking quickly at the word card and giving it another try.

6. *Concentration:* Make a duplicate set of cards so that you have two copies of each word. Be sure that the words cannot be read through the back of the card. Use 5 to 10 words and their duplicates to play a game of concentration or memory. Turn all the words face down and take turns turning two up at a time. If you turn up a matched pair, read the word and put the set in your played pile. Unmatched pairs are turned face down before the next turn.

7. *Word sorting:* Look through your child's word bank for words that share some similarity, whether in meaning, spelling pattern, or sound. Prepare a collection for sorting by pulling out two or more related groups, and then have your child sort the word-bank cards into these groups (see Figure 4.3). Some possible groupings are

FIGURE 4.3. Word-bank sorts.

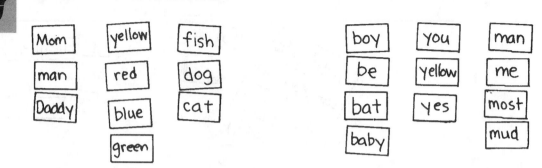

Variations for Word-Bank Review	■ Concept sorts: people words, animal words, color words, action words, happy words, little words, big words, things in a house, things outside, and so on.
	■ Sound sorts: words that begin with particular sounds such as "b" words or "m" words, words that rhyme, or words that share the same vowel sound or ending sound.
	■ Pattern sorts: words that begin with two consonants (consonant blends or digraphs) versus words that begin with single consonants.

Managing the Growing Word Bank

As your child's collection of known words grows, you may find that she will have too many word cards to be stored in a plastic baggy or to review all at one time. As a general rule, word banks are discontinued when a child has 100 or more known words. Several schemes for organizing word banks are described in Chapter 2. Of practical concern is having a means for finding out whether a particular word is already in the word bank. Rather than leafing through a stack of cards, it is easier to simply glance at an alphabetized list. It takes only a few seconds to write each new word on the Alphabetized Word-Bank List provided in Appendix A (page 138). Asking your child to spell the words for you as you write will increase the familiarity of the word for her. As the word bank grows, it is best to organize it by beginning sounds and then later by medial vowel sounds. Later, it can be converted into a personal dictionary by creating an alphabet book, writing in the new words your child is learning under the appropriate letters.

From the child's point of view, the most important thing about the word bank is its size. The number of words a child knows is like money in the bank, and we all like to see that bankroll grow. Everyone enjoys measuring success in a concrete way. For children struggling with learning to read, the positive feedback provided from a graphic display of word growth is especially important. Record the number of word-bank words your child knows on a regular basis using the record forms in Appendix A of a rocket ship or the path to the top of a mountain. You might plan a special reward for your child when he reaches 100 words, such as a colorful pencil, eraser, certificate, or book. In some schools, children reaching the 100 mark join the "Hundreds Club," and their names are announced on the loudspeaker or added to a special list posted in the hall.

What to Do When Children Forget Words

Emergent readers will frequently be able to name a word one day and not the next, so don't be surprised when this happens. If your child cannot identify a word, open the book to the page on which the word appears and ask your child to find the word. Usually, the child can use the familiar context to name the word. The word card is compared to the word in the text to make sure they match. This activity encourages the child to look closely at all the letters in the word, increasing the likelihood that it will be remembered.

If your child doesn't recognize words out of context, be patient. Ask the child to go back to the text to find a few of the unknown words in one lesson. This process is slow and can be tedious if used for more than two or three words in a row. Be prepared to discard a word if it continues to be a problem. Remember that the word bank should consist of *known* words. Also consider the possibility that you might be adding too many words at one time, or that they have not been reviewed regularly.

The word bank is important but it shouldn't take more than 5 minutes of the lesson. If you find that you are spending too much time here, alternate between gathering new words one day and reviewing the word bank on another day.

Observation Guide for the Word Bank

Ask yourself the following questions to assess how well your student did. Record your observations on the lesson plan as a guide for future planning.

- How many new words were added to the word bank?
- How did you review the word bank?
- Can your child read the vast majority of words in the word bank?
- Can she use the original context to figure out those she doesn't know?
- Which words continue to pose problems, and might you discard them?
- How many words does your child have in her word bank?

Evaluating Yourself as a Tutor on the Word Bank

After your first few tutoring sessions, evaluate your word-bank finesse by asking yourself the following questions:

- Do I let my child select new words or review words each session?
- Do I keep the word-bank record up to date and check it to see if any words were already in the word bank?
- Do I only make word cards for the words my child knows immediately?
- Do I try to include word-bank review as often as possible in each lesson?
- Do I ask my child to find a few of the unknown words in the story?
- Do I quietly discard any words my child does not know after several reviews?

Phonics

The phonics portion of word study immediately follows the word-bank work and takes another 5–7 minutes. The phonics activities focus on sounds, letters, and spelling patterns. Although the focus of the phonics lessons varies, the instructional activities follow a set routine. First, children sort picture or word cards into categories of sound with corresponding letters or letter patterns. This is called a *picture sort* or a *word sort*. After the word sort, children engage in a *writing sort*. In a writing sort, children are asked to write some of the words they just sorted. Finally, children are given letter cards to do a *"Push It Say It"* activity (Blachman, Ball, Black, & Tangle, 1994). Children learn in a concrete way how to blend pieces of words together. At first, the words are divided into two parts: the beginning sound and the word-family rhyme that follows. Beginning sounds or rhyme patterns are exchanged with other beginning sounds or rhyme patterns to illustrate concretely how to make new words. Later, words are divided into individual letters. The sample lesson with these three steps in the phonics portion of the lesson can be seen on page 63.

In this part of the plan, you will be encountering terms such as "consonants," "digraphs," "short vowels," and so forth. These phonics terms are described in the text with examples, and you can refer to the glossary in the back of the book. You should also read the background information on long and short vowels in Chapter 5.

What you will be teaching your child depends very much on what your child already knows, as demonstrated in the initial assessments. Not all children begin in the same place or progress at the same rate. As a tutor, you can tailor the phonics instruction to your child's individual needs. Only one-on-one instruction can really do this. In general, the sequence for phonics instruction for the emergent reader begins with alphabet and beginning letter–sounds, and ends with the study of vowel sounds in the middle of words. Children often can be working on two features at a time. This sequence is listed as follows:

Sequence of Phonics Instruction

1. Alphabet recognition and writing.

2. Beginning sounds (note that 1 and 2 overlap; children can work on both at the same time).

3. Short vowel rhyming word families.

4. Consonant digraphs and blends (note that 3 and 4 overlap).

5. Short vowel sounds in nonrhyming words (note that 4 and 5 overlap).

Remember that where you begin and how fast you move through this sequence depends on what your child already knows, and how easily he masters what you work on. The section below will help you make decisions about what kind of phonics instruction to plan during the word-study portion of the plan. Your child's knowledge and use of phonics will be enhanced if you can find reading materials that contain examples of the sounds you are studying. A list of books by phonic elements as well as levels can be found in Appendix B.

Alphabet Activities

If your child knows about 20 lowercase letters (out of 26), then work on the alphabet can be addressed incidentally during reading and writing. On the other hand, if your child knows less than half of the lowercase letters, she will benefit from direct, systematic work with letters both while reading and writing, as well as in isolation using game-like activities. An alphabet strip for identification and for proper letter formation should always be available for reference. If your child is trying to write something and can't remember what a letter looks like (not unusual for beginners) she can refer to the strip before her. The alphabet strip we use can be found in Appendix A (page 135). It can be attached to the tutoring box or planning folder.

Incidental Alphabet Activities. Keep in mind the particular letters that are a problem for your child and talk about them when you find them in the reading materials. You might say something like this: "Look at the title of this book. Can you find the letter 'w' in two places?" or "I want you to point to all the 'l's' on this page."

As you or your child writes, focus on problem letters by making statements such as "You'll need a lowercase 'g' to write the word 'girl.' Can you find it on the alphabet strip?"

Direct Alphabet Activities. If your child knows fewer than 20 lower case letters, you need to teach the alphabet directly using the following activities:

1. *Start with the child's name:* A good starting place for children who do not know many letters is to work on the letters in their names. Names are particularly meaningful to a child. (If your child knows the letters in his first name, work on those in his last name or a friend's name.) Write each letter of the child's name on a separate card (as shown in Figure 4.4). Lay the cards out in order and name them. You might use capitals in one row and ask the child to match lowercase letters in another row below. Scramble the letters, and have the child reassemble them, naming them as he does so. Have the child name the letters again, backward and forward, as he touches them.

FIGURE 4.4. Name cards for alphabet work.

FIGURE 4.5. Letters in ABC order.

2. *Recite the alphabet:* Find out if your child can recite the letters of the alphabet. Ask her to touch each letter on an alphabet strip or chart as she says it. You might teach her to sing the ABC song, but include touching the letters as well as singing them.

3. *Arrange the letters in order:* When your student knows 15 letters or more, she can work on putting a set of letters in alphabetical order from "a "to "z" (see Figure 4.5). Use a set of letter cards (see Appendix A), letter cutouts, link letters, magnetic letters, and so forth. Use both capital and lowercase letters. You might put the capitals in order while the child works to match the lowercase letters. The child who is weak on a number of letters should be allowed to refer to an alphabet strip. If this activity seems overwhelming or time consuming, divide the alphabet into halves or thirds.

4. *Memory or concentration:* Use the letters in the child's name, or any other letters you are working on, to play memory or concentration. Make two sets of letters so you can match lowercase to lowercase, uppercase to uppercase, or lowercase to uppercase. To keep the game fast and satisfying, don't use more than 10 pairs, or 20 letters. This is a good game, because the child has an excellent chance of winning. Turn all the letters face down to start. Players turn over any two cards at a time. If a player turns up a matching set, she must name them correctly in order to keep them.

5. *Use alphabet books:* Look up the letter(s) you are studying in an alphabet book or picture dictionary to find things that begin with that letter.

6. *Make an alphabet book:* You can create an alphabet book by stapling together blank sheets of paper and assigning a letter to each page. The top of each page is headed by the letter (in both upper- and lowercase). A personal alphabet book can be used in a number of ways for the child who needs to learn letters:

a. Encourage the child to practice writing upper- and lowercase forms of the letter.

b. Decide on the key picture that is spelled with that sound. You or the child can draw it, cut it from a magazine to paste in, or generate it from computer clip art.

c. Draw other things that begin with the letter. (Look up things in an ABC book or picture dictionary. Asking your child to think of words that begin with a particular letter is difficult if he has not learned the sound and letter matches.)

d. Add word-bank words to the alphabet book to create a dictionary of known words.

e. Use the consonant sound chart (Appendix A, page 135) or a handmade alphabet book as a point of reference to remind children of the letter–sound matches. For example,

> Malcom is reading a book from Level 3 for the second time. He comes to the word "could." He stops, staring at the word for what seems like minutes. Stanley says, "What sound goes with the letter?" Malcolm hisses out "ssssseeee" (the "letter name" of "c") and still cannot get the word. Stanley adds, "This word starts the same way as this picture of the cow on your consonant chart. What sound is that?" Malcolm changes his "see" to a "kuh." Stanley says, "Let's try reading this again, Malcolm, and show me how you can use that sound to say that tricky word." Malcolm rereads the sentence, this time reading every word correctly.

7. *Record progress:* Record the letters your child knows by coloring in the letters on the alphabet sheet in Appendix A or marking them in some other way. This will give you and your child a record of what has been learned and what still needs to be accomplished. Part of your daily routine can be going over all the known letters, gradually adding new ones as you work on them together.

Teaching the Beginning Letter–Sounds

A good way to begin teaching letter–sounds is through simple *picture sorting*. Picture sorting is a concrete, hands-on activity for comparing and categorizing sounds and matching them with letters. Children sort the picture cards into groups that all start with the same sound by placing them in columns headed with the letter that represents that sound. A key picture that is used consistently to illustrate that particular letter–sound is also useful. Materials that come in handy for phonics instruction are described in Chapter 2. Picture sorting is followed up in each session by (1) adding any word-bank words that begin with the same sounds, (2) a writing sort, and (3) a "Push It Say It" activity. These are all described below and are for use with children who need work on beginning consonant sounds.

Picture Sorting with Beginning Sounds.   When you are working with letter–sounds, you will first help your child attend to beginning sounds with activities such as picture sorting. Picture sorts always contrast *at least two* sounds at the same time. A good starting point is sorting pictures of objects that start with "m" and "s." These sounds are very different from each other and can be said slowly, without distortion.

1. Use letter cards to head each category (see Figure 4.6). Select a key picture for each sound (such as "mouse" and "sun") and put them under the corresponding letter to start a sorting column. You can emphasize and elongate the beginning sound by stretching it out.

FIGURE 4.6. Picture sort of "s" and "m," with several words at bottom.

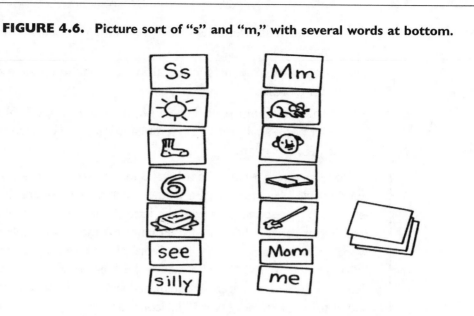

2. Shuffle the rest of the picture cards and say to the child something like "We are going to listen for the sound at the beginning of these words and decide if they begin like 'mouse' or like 'sun.' I'll do a few first. Here is a sock. Sssock begins like sssun so I'll put it under the letter 's' and the picture of the sun. It starts with an 's.' Here is a man. Mmmman begins like mmmmouse, so I'll put it under the 'm.' Now it is your turn. You pick a card and decide where to put it."

3. After modeling several pictures, turn the task over to the child or take turns as you sort the rest of the collection. If the child makes a mistake, correct it immediately. Simply say "'Six' would go under 'sun.' It starts with an 's'." Your child may not know what to call a picture. Simply tell her what it is. If she continues to have trouble naming it, just eliminate it from the deck. Don't make naming the pictures into a guessing game. You can include words from the child's word bank in these sorts as well.

4. After completing the first sort with your help, immediately ask your child to sort again, but this time independently and as fast as she can. Don't neglect to ask her to name each picture aloud as she sorts.

5. Do not correct her this time during the sorting, but when she is through, have her name the pictures in each column to check herself. If there are misplaced cards that she fails to find, tell her how many, and ask her to try and find them herself.

Further Studies of Beginning Sounds Picture Sorts.   If your student can easily sort "m" and "s," you can add "b" words and then "r" words over the next two sessions until you have four categories of initial sounds. Repeat this kind of sequence with all the letters, working with up to four categories at a time. The particular sequence is not too important, but a suggested one is shown below for children who need a lot of work on beginning sounds. If your child used most of the consonants in the spelling inventory correctly, a quick review that compares four sounds at a time over 4 or 5 weeks is all that may be needed.

If your child only missed one or two consonant sounds, be selective about the letters you work on. For example, your child might have confused "v" and "f" on the spelling of "van" as "fn." An appropriate sort for that child would be to compare pictures of words that start with "v" and words that start with "f." Do not linger too long on initial sounds if your child is able to sort them accurately and quickly. As you work with same-vowel word families you will also review consonant sounds.

Suggested Sequence for Initial Consonant Sound Sorting	(1) M/S, M/S/B, M/S/B/R	(2) P/N, P/N/T, P/N/T/G
	(3) C/F, C/F/D, C/F/D/H	(4) J/L, J/K/L, J/K/L/W
	(5) V/Y/Z	(6) SH/S/H, CH/J/H, TH/CH/SH/WH

Include picture sorting of words that begin with short vowels if you have pictures to use, mixing them in with the consonants. Words such as "apple" and "ax" are good to use for the beginning short "a." "Octopus" and "ox" are good for short "o." Avoid words such as "elephant" or "Indian" because children are likely to confuse the beginning sound with "l" (elephant) and "n" (Indian).

After the study of single consonants, it is appropriate to teach beginning *consonant digraphs: sh, th, wh,* and *ch.* These consonant digraphs are quite common and behave like single consonants in that they represent a single sound. We recommend comparing single consonants to their corresponding digraphs using picture cards. For example, we might compare pictures of a "sun," "sail," or "sink" with pictures of a "shoe," "ship," or "shirt." Of course, we would head each category with the corresponding letters "s" or *sh*. Pictures beginning with *ch* might be compared with pictures that start with "c," and pictures that start with "h," because young writers often confuse those sounds and letters.

Word Sorts for Beginning Sounds. Phonics is all about the systematic correspondence between letters and sounds. Because of this, it is important to add word-bank words to each of the picture sorts described earlier. After sorting the picture cards into categories headed by the corresponding letters, pull out your child's word bank and give him those words that start with the same letter–sounds. This is easy if you have arranged the word bank into pockets as suggested in Chapter 2. Let him sort the word cards into the correct categories, naming each word as he does so.

Writing Sorts for Beginning Sounds. In writing sorts, children are asked to write a few words as part of the phonics portion of the lesson plan. Writing sorts strengthen the connection between sounds and letters.

1. You or the child should first write the beginning sounds you have been studying at the top of the paper to serve as headers for the lists of written words.

2. Select several pictures from the sort you have just completed. Generally, two pictures for each sound will be enough. Scramble the pictures and turn them face down.

3. Invite your child to turn over a card and then attempt to write as much of the word as she can. Since you have been working on the initial consonant sound, that is all that you can really expect the child to write correctly. Children can be encouraged to listen for and write more sounds in the word, but don't expect these additional sounds to be correct.

Here is how Stanley worked with Malcolm on a writing sort.

> "Malcolm, let's see if you can spell some words now. Open up your notebook to a clean page and write "m," "r," and "s" at the top. *(While Malcolm gets ready, Stanley picks out six pictures and lays them face down on the table.)* Pick out one of these words to spell. *(Malcolm turns over the picture of a mouse, and he writes down an "m" under the letter "m" in his notebook.)* That's good, fella, but can you hear some more sounds in that word? Say it slowly like this, mmmoussse. *(Malcolm echoes what Stanley has done and adds an "s" to spell "mouse" as ms.)* That will do. What are you going to spell next? *(Malcolm turns over a picture of a road. After being encouraged to say it slowly, he writes rod.)* That's great Malcolm. You put in the sound in the middle too."

"Push It Say It" Procedures for Beginning Sounds. Throughout the study of beginning sounds, children need practice manipulating the beginning sound and exchanging one sound for another to make a new word. This skill will eventually help them sound out unfamiliar words as they read by blending sounds and word parts together. For example, if your child has been sorting pictures and word-bank words beginning with "s," "m," and "f," you might choose the word "sat" for a "Push It Say It" activity.

1. Create letter cards or copy and cut out the letters you will need from the letter cards in Appendix A (for example, cut out the "s," "m," and "f" letters, as well as the AT card from the word-family cards).

2. Push the "s" card up on the table while saying "s-s-s." Next, push the AT card next to it while saying "at." Push the cards together and say the word "sat."

3. Tell your child that you can take the "s" away and change the word into "mat." Push the "m" card up a little further, saying "m-m-m." Then push the AT card next to it saying "at." Then say "mat."

FIGURE 4.7. "Push It Say It" with "s" and AT.

4. After modeling this procedure, ask your child to push and say "sat," take away the "s," then push and say the two parts of "mat."

5. Repeat with one or two other beginning sounds to make "mat" into "fat." If your child does not "push and say" the letter cards correctly, help him by guiding his "push" while he says the sounds. If he *does* succeed, show him how to change the word "sat" into "mat" by exchanging the "s" card for the "m" card.

Introducing Short Vowels

If your child consistently represents beginning and final sounds but does not consistently include a vowel in the middle of words, you will start your phonics instruction with rhyming word families that have the same short vowel. Work with word families encourages children to think of the vowel and the letter(s) that follow (such as the AT in "cat" or the ACK in "back") as a *rhyming chunk* that always "says the same thing." Most of the words you will use at first will be simple, three-letter words that serve as a review of consonants. But word family study can also be used to reinforce consonant digraphs (*sh, th, ch, wh*) and to introduce consonant blends (such as *tr, bl, st*, etc.).

The particular word family that you decide to study will depend on the words that your child has in her word bank and the words she is encountering in her reading. The AT family or the AN family is often a good place to start, since "cat," "man," and "can" occur in many beginning books. Your child should know several words in each family before you work with that family. These known words will serve as the starting point for reading the others.

Comparing Same-Vowel Rhyming Word Families.   The following sorting activity can be used to introduce rhyming word families that share the same vowel. It should be followed by a writing sort and a "Push It Say It" exercise. Lists of words to use for these sorts can be found in Appendix A, page 140.

Basic Sorting Procedure for Same-Vowel Word Families.   The procedure described here will guide you through the steps of a word family sort and need to be followed carefully (see Figure 4.8).

1. Prepare word cards for sorting (for example: "cat," "hat," "mat," "sat," "pat," and "rat" to compare with "can," "man," "fan," "ran," and "van"). Be sure that your child can read one or two of the words in each family (typically those would be "cat" and "man"). Start with three-letter words but add at least a few words with digraphs and blends later on (for example, "that," "chat," "flat").

2. Lay down a known word to start each category (for example, "cat" and "man") and shuffle the rest of the words.

3. Turn over a card and place it under the header word that rhymes. Read the header word and the new word (for example, "cat," "rat").

FIGURE 4.8. Word-family sort with AT and AN.

4. Model two or three words in this fashion, each time reading down from the top before reading the new word (for example, "cat," "rat," "sat").

5. Now, invite the child to do the next word. The child should sort it first and then read all the words from the top down before attempting the new word. This will enable the child to use rhyme to support her effort to read the new words. If your child has difficulty reading a new word, you can prompt her by saying "Say the first sound."

6. After all the words have been sorted, ask your child how the words in each column are alike. You want your child to pay attention to common sounds, letters, and the position of those letters. Probe for answers such as "They rhyme" or "They all have an 'a' and a 't' in them." Explain that the words in each column are called a family because they all end with "a" and "t." Words that rhyme often have the same spelling pattern.

7. Ask your child to sort again independently, reading from the top as each new word is added.

Further Studies of Word Families. The first word families that are compared should share the same short vowel, as in AT and AN earlier. Start by just comparing two and then try three or four different families at a time, adding new ones to the ones you have already studied so that they are reviewed. A suggested sequence is listed below, but remember that your choice may vary depending on the words your child knows and the words that show up in the reading material. There really is no reason why you couldn't start by comparing OG words with OT words, or any other family.

Learning the first few short vowel rhyming families may go slowly, but most children will begin to need much less reinforcement with later families as they transfer their learning to new vowels and rhyming chunks. There is no reason to study every one. Even the suggested list below has more sorts than many children will need. To really help children learn the vowels, you will need to compare word families with different vowels and words that are not in families. These sorts are described in the next few sections.

Possible Sequence for the Study of Word Families with the Same Vowel	Short A families:	1. -AT and -AN	(Start with two families.)
		2. -AP and -AT	(Add another and review one.)
		3. -AT, -AG, -AP	(Try three, but include a familiar one for review.)
		4. -AN, -AD, -AP, -ACK	(Try four, but include some familiar ones.)
	Short I families:	5. -IG, -IT, -IP	(Start with two or maybe three on the second short vowel you tackle.)
		6. -IN, -ID, -ILL, -ICK	(Be ready to pick up the pace whenever you can.)

(*Note:* At this point, you could continue with sorts that have the same short vowel, or you could begin contrasting vowels by comparing word families such as AT and IT, or IP and AP.)

	Short O families:	7. -OT, -OG, -OP, -OCK	(You might be able to start off with four, but drop back to two or three, if needed.)
	Short E families:	8. -ET, -EN, -ED, -ELL	(It should be getting easy by now to do three or four at a time.)
	Short U families:	9. -UT, -UG, -UCK, -UMP	

Writing Sort for Same-Vowel Word Families.   The writing sort for word families is similar to that for beginning sounds, except that now you can expect your child to spell the entire word correctly.

1. Set up the headers for the categories you will need by writing a key word at the top of each column. These might be "cat," "man," and "sad" (see Figure 4.9).

2. Call out two or three words in each category for the child to spell. If you call out "mad," he should write it under the word "sad."

3. Assist your child when needed by saying the word slowly, drawing out the sounds, and stressing each one: mmmm-aaaa-t. Ask your child to say each word too.

4. As soon as the word is written, show the word card for your child to self-check. There is no reason to erase an error. Just ask your child to draw a line through it and write it again in the correct column.

FIGURE 4.9. Writing sort for word families AT, AN, and AD order.

"Push It Say It" for Same-Vowel Word Families. "Push It Say It" routines for same-vowel word families teach children to pay attention to the vowel and the letters that follow, and to treat these letters as a chunk that can be peeled off and combined with other beginning sounds to make new words. The steps are similar to what they were for beginning sounds, but you will vary the ending chunk.

1. Choose the beginning letter and rhyme cards in Appendix A (pages 141–143) that match the word sorts you have just done. If you have been working with the AT and AN families, cut out these rhyme chunks as well as an assortment of beginning sounds such as "m," "s," and "f." Two or three rhyme chunks are enough for one sitting.

2. Push the "m" card up on the table while saying "m-m-m." Next, push the AT card next to it while saying "at." Push the cards together and say the word "mat."

3. Tell your child that you can take the "at" away and change the word into "man." Push the "m" card up a little further, saying "m-m-m," then push the AN card next to it saying "an." Then say "man."

4. After modeling this procedure, ask your child to push and say "mat," take away the "at," then push and say the two parts of "man."

5. Repeat with one or two other beginning sounds to make "sat" into "sad" and "fan" into "fat."

Comparing Mixed-Vowel Rhyming Word Families. If children used short vowels to spell words on the initial assessment but used the wrong short vowels, they may have created efforts that look like this: PAT for "pet," ROG for "rug," PLOM for "plum." You can start your phonics instruction with mixed-vowel families that compare different short vowels. Since young spellers often get the short "a" correct but confuse the others, it makes sense to start by comparing something known (short "a" families) with something unknown or often

FIGURE 4.10. Mixed-vowel word sort.

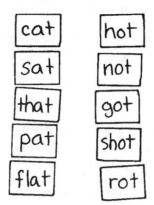

confused (such as short "o" word families). A sample mixed-vowel sort is shown in Figure 4.10.

Basic Sorting Procedure for Mixed-Vowel Word Families.

1. Set up headers such as "cat" for the AT words and "hot" for the OT words.

2. Model the sorting of several words, reading the header first and then the new word.

3. Invite the child to sort the next word and then ask him to read from the header down to the new word.

4. After the words are sorted, ask the child how the words in each category are alike.

5. Ask the child to sort again on his own.

Possible Sequence for the Study of Mixed-Vowel Word Families

1. -AT and -OT (Start with two families.)

2. -IT, -AT, -OT (Add another family with a different vowel.)

3. -IT, -OT, -UT, -ET (Try four, but include some for review. Be ready to go back to two or three if this is difficult.)

4. -AN, -IN, -AP, -IP (Mix up different vowels and ending consonants.)

5. -AD, -AG, -ID, -IG

6. -IG, -OG, -UG, -EG

7. -OP, -UP, -OCK, -UCK

8. -ACK, -OCK, -ICK, -UCK (Remember to include words with blends and digraphs such as "*black*" and "*shack*.")

9. -ALL, -ELL, -ILL
(Try other combinations depending on the words you encounter in the materials you read. The chart of common word families in Appendix A will give you other ideas as well.)

Writing Sort for Mixed-Vowel Word Families.   The procedure is exactly like the procedure for same-vowel families.

1. Set up the headers for the categories you will need by writing a key word at the top of each column. These might be "cat," "not," and "sit."

2. Call out two or three words in each category for the child to spell. If you call out "hot," she should write it under the word "not."

3. Assist your child, when needed, by saying the word slowly, drawing out the sounds, and stressing each one. Ask your child to say the word.

4. As soon as the word is written, show the word card for your child to self-check. Errors should be crossed out and rewritten in the correct category.

"Push It Say It" for Mixed-Vowel Word Families.   "Push It Say It" routines for mixed-vowel families teach children to pay attention to the vowel in the middle. With practice, children see that medial vowel sounds are crucial to identify words. The procedure is very similar to the "Push It Say It" for same-vowel word families. Include any blends or digraphs you have worked on. Blends and digraphs cards are included in the "Push It Say It" materials in Appendix A. Note that a digraph such as SH is on *one* card, not separated into an S card and an H card.

1. Choose the letter and rhyme card in Appendix A (pages 141–143) that matches the word sort you have just done. If you have been working with the AP, OP, and IP families, cut out these rhyme chunks as well as two or three beginning sounds such as SH, CH, and T.

2. Push the SH card up on the table while saying "shshshshs." Next, push the OP card next to it while saying "op." Finally, say the word "shop."

3. Tell your child that you can take the "op" away and change the word into "ship." Push the SH card up a little further, saying "shshshsh." Then, push the IP card next to it, saying "ip." Then, say "ship."

4. After modeling this procedure, ask your child to push and say "shop," take away the "op," then push and say the two parts of "ship."

5. Repeat with one or two other beginning sounds to change "tip" to "tap" and "top" or "chip" to "chop" and "chap."

Teaching the Beginning Blends.   Consonant blends are two consonants that are blended together, such as the "c" and "l" in the word "clock." We can still distinguish each separate sound, but the two letters work together as a tightly meshed sound unit. Most consonant blends occur at the beginning of words, and it is on this position that we focus our attention. Blends may be studied through picture sorts (see Figure 4.11). For example, pictures starting with "s" may be contrasted with pictures starting with SC, SK, SL, SM, SN, SP, or SW. "S" blends are probably the easiest of the blends and make a good starting point. "R" blends (BR, CR, DR, FR, GR, TR) and "l" blends (BL, CL, FL, GL, SL) are more difficult. Like all picture sorts, each column should be headed by a

🕴 **FIGURE 4.11.** Picture sort with blends.

card with the letters being taught (S versus ST, for example). Also add word-bank words, that start with S and ST.

The study of blends should also take place during the study of word families by including blends with short vowel rhyming words. For example, the -AT family can be expanded to include "flat," "scat," or "brat." Words with blends should be included in the basic sorting activities as well as the "Push It Say It" routine and writing sorts. For the "Push It Say It" routine, select cards that have blends from the letter cards in Appendix A. For example, you might pick ST, SN, SM, and SL to use with -ACK. Push the ST card up on the table while saying "sssst." Next, push the ACK card next to it while saying "ack." Finally, say the word "stack." Repeat to create "snack," "smack," and "slack."

Comparing Nonrhyming Short Vowels.   When children are showing great facility with rhyming word families, move to nonrhyming word sorting to focus on short vowels in isolation. You should begin by sorting pictures by the short vowel sound as shown in the sort in Figure 4.12. Words from your child's word bank can be added, as well as words you used in the word family sorts described earlier.

Basic Sorting Procedure for Nonrhyming Short Vowel Words.

1. Use picture cards or prepare word cards for sorting that your child can already read. Look through your child's word bank for words with the short vowel sound you are studying.

2. Lay down a header to start each category (for example, "sack," "pot," and "pig," as shown in the sample) and shuffle the rest of the words.

3. Turn over a card, name it, or read it, and place it under the header word with the same vowel. You can isolate the vowel sound by "peeling" off the first and last consonants like this: "sack" "ack" "a."

4. Invite your child to do the next word. Your child should name it first and then sort the word. It is no longer necessary to read down from the top each

FIGURE 4.12. Picture sort of nonrhyming short vowels with several words at the bottom.

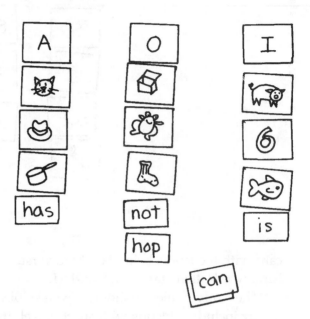

time. If your child has difficulty sorting, have her isolate the vowel as described in Step 3.

6. After all the words or pictures have been sorted, read down from the top, checking to see that all the words have the same vowel sound. Ask your child how the words in each column are alike. (They all have the same short "a" sound.)

7. Ask the child to sort again, as quickly as she can.

Writing Sort for Nonrhyming Short Vowel Words. The procedure for writing sorts is very similar to writing word families, and the entire word should be spelled correctly.

1. Set up the headers for the categories you will need by writing a short vowel at the top each column. These might be "a," "o," and "i."

2. Call out two or three words in each category for the child to spell. If you call out "hot," he should write it under "o."

3. Assist your child when needed by saying the word slowly, drawing out the sounds and stressing each one. Ask your child to say the word also.

4. As soon as the word is written, show the word card for your child to self-check. Errors should be crossed out and rewritten in the correct category.

"Push It Say It" for Nonrhyming Short Vowel Words. "Push It Say It" routines for medial vowels focus attention on the short vowel sound in the middle of the word. The procedure changes slightly for nonfamily words, because you will be pushing *three* cards instead of two (see Figure 4.13). Choose three letter

FIGURE 4.13. "Push It Say It" with three letter cards.

cards from Appendix A that, when put together, will make a three-letter word. You will need a consonant, several vowels, and another consonant (for example, "o," "e," "u," and "n" and "t"). Be sure that the vowel letters you choose match the short vowel sounds in picture and word sorts you have just done. Two or three words are enough for one sitting, as shown in this example:

1. Choose vowel letters that match the word sorts you have just done (such as "a," "i," and "o") as well as two consonant sounds (such as "n" and "t").

2. Push the "n" card up on the table while saying "n-n-n." Next, push the "o" card next to it while saying "o-o-o" (as in "octopus"). Finally, push the "t" card up while saying "t," then say the word "not."

3. Tell your child that you can take the "o" away and change the word into "net." Push the "n" card up a little further, saying "n-n-n." then push the "e" card next to it, saying "eh-eh-eh" (as in Eskimo). Then, push the "t" card up once again, saying "t." Then, say "net."

4. Repeat the same procedure, substituting the "u" to make "nut."

5. After modeling this procedure, ask your child to push and say the three letter sounds of "not," "net," and "nut."

Some other combinations to try for nonfamily short vowel "Push It Say It" practice are listed below. Use letter cards with blends and digraphs as well. These are included in Appendix A (pages 141–143). To push and say "clock," you would need three cards: CL, O, and CK. CL is a blend of sounds and CK is a digraph that has only one sound. Both blends and digraphs are treated as a unit in "Push It Say It" activities.

"Push It Say It" Suggestions for Nonrhyming Short Vowels			
	fan, fin, fun	sack, sick, sock	pat, pet, pit, pot
	cat, cot, cut	slap, slip, slop	hat, hit, hot, hut
	net, not, nut	chap, chip, chop	bat, bet, bit, but
	jig, jog, jug	clap, clip, clop	tack, tick, tock, tuck
	tap, tip, top	track, trick, truck	lack, lick, lock, lock
	cap, cop, cup	stack, stick, stuck	clack, click, clock, cluck
	rat, rot, rut	bag, beg, big, bog, bug	ham, him, hum

Observation Guide for the Phonics Part of the Lesson Plan

Ask yourself the following questions to assess how well your student did in the phonics portion of word study. Record your observations in the comments section of the lesson plan as a guide for future planning.

▪ How well was your child able to sort the pictures or words? (Sorting should be quick and sure after the first time or two.)

▪ Should you repeat the sort again or move on to new categories at your next session?

▪ Should you drop back and have fewer categories next time, or can you increase the number of categories? (No more than 4 at a time is a general rule.)

▪ Was your child able to spell the words in the writing sort accurately?

▪ Is your child able to follow your lead in doing the "Push It Say It" activity and blend the new words together?

Evaluating Yourself as a Tutor on the Phonics Part of the Lesson Plan

After completing the phonics portion of word study, you might check yourself on the following points. If you answer negatively to any of them, don't give up; try again next time! Phonics instruction is very complex, and you and your child may be learning it together.

▪ Do I keep track of unknown alphabet letters and direct my child's attention to them?

▪ Do I set up the category headers and model the first card or two when introducing new categories?

▪ Do I hand the cards to my child to sort after modeling several?

▪ Do I make sure my child names each word aloud during sorting, and when my child doesn't recognize a picture, do I immediately tell her what it is?

▪ Do I remain silent during the second sort and allow my student to make mistakes?

▪ As a conclusion to my sort, do I have my child read down each column to help her find and correct mistakes, and do I ask what all the words have in common?

▪ Does my child sort the words or pictures at least twice?

▪ Do I include the writing sort and the "Push It Say It" activity every time?

▪ During the phonics portion of the lesson, am I well prepared, so we can move quickly through all the activities nearly every lesson?

We have just presented a lot of information about phonics and spelling instruction. But remember, the child won't be doing it all at once. It will take time to move from beginning sounds to short vowels in the middle. The entire word study section of the plan, including word-bank work, should not take more than 10–12 minutes. Don't overdo it! Watch your time.

Emergent Reader Lesson Plan
Part III: Writing for Sounds

The writing component of the emergent reader lesson plan is referred to as "writing for sounds" and should take only 5–10 minutes. Children's understanding of letters and sounds is further enhanced through this activity. Writing demands that children segment, or divide, their speech into sounds and match those segmented sounds to letters. You will often need to model the segmentation process by stretching out the sounds in the words and then encourage your child to do the same. This kind of writing exercises beginning readers' phonics knowledge in a meaningful way.

The writing can take a variety of forms, as described below, but is usually limited to a single sentence. We hope your child has the opportunity to write extensively and freely on topics of interest to himself in the classroom, where more time can be allotted to this activity. The creative writing process is beyond the scope of these tutoring sessions.

The sentence you use for writing may grow out of the word study portion of the lesson plan, or it may repeat words from a story you have been reading. Whether the sentence is created by the child, the tutor, or collaboratively, your job is to repeat the sentence word by word as the child spells as best he or she can. Below are some examples for each type of dictated sentence:

1. *Story-based sentences:* A story-based sentence comes from, or is suggested by, a book the child has recently read. You might choose a sentence from the book that either repeats or summarizes the story. Stanley chose "I saw a lion at the zoo," and Malcolm's writing looked like this: *I S a Lin at the zoo.* In past tutoring sessions, Malcolm had sorted beginning consonant sounds but had not yet worked with vowels. He remembered the vowels in the word "zoo," which has a distinctive visual appearance, and the "e" in "the," which he knows as a sight word. Stanley did not expect him to get any more of the word "saw," but he did say "lion" slowly and asked Malcolm to listen for a sound in the middle. With this help, Malcolm was able to add an "i."

2. *Personal sentences:* A personal sentence reflects something of interest to the child: new shoes, a snowy day, a new pet, and so forth. If your child volunteers some personal news before or during your tutoring session, take advantage of the occasion. Decide upon a sentence that summarizes the news, and use it for the dictation. For example, one day Malcolm came in excited about sleeping over at his cousin's house. Together, he and Stanley decided upon the following sentence: "I like to sleep at Larry's house." Malcolm's writing looked like this: *I like to sep at Larry's hs.* The word "like" was spelled correctly because Malcolm remembered it was in his word bank, and he looked it up on the word-bank list. Stanley helped him spell his cousin's name correctly and showed him how to put the -'s at the end.

3. *Word study–based sentences:* A word study sentence uses word-bank words or phonics features such as rhyming word families. When Malcolm begins the study of digraphs, Stanley might dictate a sentence such as "She sells sea shells." When Malcolm studies consonant blends and the ACK family, he might be given the following sentence: "Pack your snack in your backpack!"

Questions Tutors Often Ask

What If My Child Doesn't Leave Spaces between the Words When She Writes?

The spaces are important, but putting them in is a common problem with young writers. Children who lack a Concept of Word can be helped by writing a separate line on the paper for each word in the dictated sentence (see Figure 4.14). Say the sentence, and ask your child to tell you the first word. Then say, "Let's write that word on the first line." Point to the next line, and say the next word. Proceed in this manner word by word, repeating the sentence from time to time. Support your child's effort by saying the words slowly, emphasizing individual sounds. Children who have a solid Concept of Word can be encouraged to place a finger space between each word they write.

What If My Child Can't Remember How to Form Some of the Letters?

Always have an alphabet strip available for reference during writing. One is included in Appendix A (page 135), but find out what system is used by the school, and ask for a copy if it is different. If your child is unsure of how to make a letter, direct her attention to the alphabet strip and help her with the correct movements. Familiarize yourself with the letter formation system used by the child's school, and use those forms yourself when you write for the child.

How Accurate Does the Child's Spelling Need to Be?

In the writing for sounds section, it is not necessary for the final product to be written in perfectly correct spelling, because these sentences will not be used as reading material. Hold your child accountable for what she has been studying during the word study portion of your lessons, but do not hold her accountable for word features she has not yet been taught. It is important that you accept

FIGURE 4.14. Writing with lines for words.

your child's best effort at a reasonable phonetic spelling, although you can always stretch your child's understanding by saying the word slowly, emphasizing additional sounds as well.

At the emergent stage, it is unreasonable to expect your child to write any silent letters unless they are in words your child has learned to spell from frequent exposure. For example, it is possible that your child might spell the word "blue" correctly, including the silent "e" on the end, because it is familiar to her. However, her efforts at spelling "road," "light," and "sheep" might look like ROD, LIT, and SHEP.

Common high-frequency words are particularly difficult for children to learn to read and spell, because they don't mean much all by themselves, and because they are often not very phonetically regular. Consider words such as "said," "was," and "of." Spelling these words by "sound" might result in phonetic efforts such as SED, WUZ, and UV. If any of these high-frequency words are in your child's word bank, you might help the child spell it correctly by pulling out that word card or pointing to it on the alphabetized word-bank list. Or you might simply write it for him to see and copy. These words are used so frequently that it makes sense just to memorize the correct spelling, so that when the word is needed for writing or encountered in reading, it can be spelled or read immediately and accurately. Since many of these words will probably be on the word-bank list, keep the list handy for reference during writing.

What about Other Conventions of Writing such as Punctuation and Capitalization?

By all means, give your child pointers about writing conventions and encourage their use, but don't expect mastery of them for some time, and don't overdo it. Don't worry about quotation marks and commas, but do remind your child to start with a capital and end each sentence with a period or question mark. Be willing to let some conventions go uncorrected, especially when you first begin working with your child.

**Observation Guide for the
Writing for Sounds Portion of the Lesson Plan**

Ask yourself the following questions to assess how well your student did in the writing for sounds portion of the lesson plan. Record your observations on the lesson plan in the comments section.

- How willing is your child to write?

- Is he able to represent the sounds in his writing that you expect?

- What help did he require from you?

- How well does your child do with the conventions of writing, such as letter formation, spaces, capitals, punctuation, and so on?

**Evaluating Yourself as a Tutor on the
Writing for Sounds Portion of the Lesson Plan**

After completing the writing for sounds portion of the lesson plan, you might check yourself on the following points.

■ Do I have a sentence ready in advance, but am I flexible if something more appropriate develops during tutoring?

■ Do I let my child do the sounding out and writing, and lend support only as needed?

■ Do I offer simple tips and suggestions when appropriate, but am I also willing to let some things "slide"?

■ Do I have reasonable expectations about what my child can write based upon the information I have from the assessment and from our progress in word study?

Emergent Reader Lesson Plan
Part IV: Introducing New Reading Materials

New reading material is introduced at the end of every tutoring session. This is a critical part of the lesson plan and should not be omitted. If you feel you are running short on time, skip the writing for sounds part (you might find you can squeeze it in later) or cut word study short, but always leave adequate time to read a new book. Time spent reading is the most important component of the lesson plan. Generally, save about 10 minutes to do this.

There are four steps to consider when introducing a book:

**Steps in a
Book
Introduction**

1. Preview the book with your child by looking at the illustrations and talking about the contents.

2. The child reads the book on her own, with assistance as needed.

3. The reading is followed by some more informal discussion.

4. The child reads the book a second time to reinforce what she has learned the first time through. (It is important to read it at least twice, and even a third time, if the child is willing and the book is short.)

The preview is important and should be planned in advance. It serves several purposes. It will stimulate your child's interest in the story as well as your child's background knowledge of the topic. We hope you will get your child talking about experiences she has had that relate to the events or characters in the story. The preview also prepares the child for a successful reading by highlighting new ideas, new words, and language patterns.

Emergent readers have a limited sight vocabulary and limited letter–sound knowledge, which makes it unlikely that they can read much of anything without some introduction. As children acquire a store of known words and strategies for using context clues, they will gradually be able to read more and more independently, and new books may require only a brief introduction. Some books will require more of an introduction than others because of unusual language or unfamiliar topics.

Selecting Books to Introduce

Book selection is the first critical step. Use the guidelines in Chapter 3 to help pinpoint an approximate reading level and then select from the available leveled books or the list in Appendix B. Also consider what phonics elements your child is working on in the word study part of the plan and look for books that have many examples of that element (see Appendix B for lists). In general, the new books will be at the same level of difficulty for several weeks before moving on to a higher level. New books should offer just the right amount of challenge. There should be a few problems to solve but not so many that the child will feel frustrated. The books you will be using for readers in the emergent stage offer a lot of support for reading through the pictures, through the patterned and repetitive language, and through the familiar settings and situations.

Preparing a Book Preview

Look through the new book before using it with your student to familiarize yourself with it and think about the support your student will need to read it independently. Try to anticipate where your child may have a problem. Decide whether he can solve it alone or whether you should prepare him for it in advance. Expect to get better at this as you get to know your child. Here are the steps in previewing a new book:

1. Read the title of the book aloud to your child as you point to the words. Often, the title will include a key word or two that will reappear in the story (for example, the Level 4 book, *I Went Walking* by Sue Williams, has the words "I went walking" throughout). Ask your child to repeat the title after you.

2. Look at the cover of the book and discuss the illustration. You might ask, "What do you see?" or "What do you think this story will be about?"

3. Offer a very brief summary of one or two sentences that tell what the book will be about and engage your child in some talk about the topic. Ask questions such as "Has that every happened to you?"; "Do you have a ___ ?"; or "Do you like ___ ?"

4. Look through the pictures in the book and talk about what the book is about as you do so. Point out objects in the pictures that correspond to the words on the page that the student will need to read (for example, point to the picture and say "That machine is called a crane, and here is the word 'crane'." Engage children in conversation about the pictures so that they use some of the words and language of the story.

TABLE 4.1. Sample Story to Introduce

My Pizza	(Cover shows Mom spreading dough in a pan.)
Put on the sauce.	(Picture shows boy spreading on red sauce.)
Put on the cheese.	(Picture shows boy sprinkling on yellow cheese.)
Put on the pepperoni.	(Picture shows boy spreading on pepperoni.)
Put it in the oven.	(Picture shows Mom pushing it in the oven.)
Cut it up	(Picture shows Mom cutting the pizza.)
and take a bite.	(Picture shows boy holding a piece with his mouth wide open.)

5. Use the vocabulary and language patterns in the story. This includes the names of characters (such as Louisa, Miguel, or Mrs. Wishy Washy) that the child is unlikely to know. If there is a sentence pattern that repeats throughout the book, work it into your introduction. If there is a change in the pattern, bring it to the child's attention.

Stanley has prepared a book preview for Malcolm using a simple story at Level 4 (see Table 4.1). Each line of the text is on a separate page and is accompanied by a picture that corresponds to the sentence. Here is how Stanley previewed the book:

Stanley: Here is a new book I think you will like. The name of the book is *My Pizza. (He points to the words in the title as he reads.)* What kind of pizza do you like?

Malcolm: I like sausage pizza and my brother likes pepperoni, so we always fight about what kind to get.

Stanley: Yeah, I like mushrooms on mine, but no one else in my family does. Have you ever made a pizza?

Malcolm: No, but we get frozen ones sometimes.

Stanley: Well this story is about a boy helping his Mom make a pizza. Look at the cover. What is Mom doing here?

Malcolm: Looks like she is making a pizza.

Stanley: Yep, she is spreading the dough out in the pan. What are they going to put on the dough? Let's look at the pictures and see how they make the pizza. What did he put on first?

Malcolm: He put on the red stuff. What is that called?

Stanley: Sauce, he put on the sauce. *(He points to the word on the page.)* Next, he put on the . . .

Malcolm: Cheese!

Stanley: Right! Where's that word? And then he put on . . . ?

Malcolm: The sausage.

Stanley: You wish! Look at this word. *(He points to "pepperoni" in the sentence.)* Can that word be sausage? What does it start with? What else could it be?

Malcolm: P. Pepperoni.

Stanley: Yeah, your brother would like this pizza. Let's look at the next page. What do you see?

Malcolm: Mom put it in the stove to cook.

Stanley: And then . . .

Malcolm: She cut it up. *(Stanley turns the page.)* And he ate it.

Stanley: Right. Now he can *take a bite. (Stanley points to those three words as he says them.)* I think you are ready to read this book called *My Pizza.* Remember to touch each word as you read.

Stanley has made sure that Malcolm knows all the words that label the ingredients, and that he has heard the language of the sentence pattern "Put on the . . ." He elicited and used the language of the last sentence, which changes the pattern and focused Malcolm's attention on the print. He has invited Malcolm to participate throughout this preview by asking questions and pausing to let Malcolm fill in the blanks. The tone is friendly and informal as Stanley commiserates and teases. A well-planned book preview includes information and questioning but should come across in practice as informal and conversational.

Observing as your child reads, and reflecting upon the problems he has, will help you plan future book previews. Over time, you will become better at anticipating potential problems and dealing with them in your previews.

Responding during Reading of a New Book

The first thing you do when your child needs help is to stop and think, and give the child time to think as well. See if you can puzzle out the source of the problem, and think about the clues you might give your child to help him solve the problem. Let's see how Stanley works with Malcolm on the first reading of *My Pizza.*

Stanley: I think you are ready to read this book called *My Pizza.* Remember to touch each word as you read.

Malcolm: *(He reads the first three pages.)* Put on the sauce. Put on the cheese. Put on the sausage . . . no, pepperoni.

Stanley: Good for you, Malcolm. How did you fix that?

Malcolm: I remembered the P.

Stanley: That's right. Pepperoni starts with P. Keep going.

Malcolm: Put on the . . . stove? *(Malcolm pauses and frowns at the sentence but then starts to turn the page.)*

Stanley: Try that again, Malcolm, and touch each word.

Malcolm: Put on . . . no, put *it* . . . in . . . the stove.

Stanley: You've almost got it. Look at this word. *(He points to "oven.")* Can that be "stove"? What is that part of the stove called? *(Malcolm doesn't seem to know and shakes his head.)*

Stanley: Could that word be "oven"?

Malcolm: Oh yeah, oven. Put it in the oven. *(He turns to the next page, which has the words "Cut it up.")* Put . . . *(He pauses and looks at Stanley.)*

Stanley: Look at the picture. What did Mom do?

Malcolm: Cut it up *(He turns to the last page)* and take a bite!

Malcolm made some mistakes and self-corrections here, and each one suggested that he was using some source of information. Read back through the previous exchange and see if you can figure out the source of his problems and corrections. The sentence "Put it in the oven" gave him the most problem. He seemed to automatically apply the same pattern from the first three sentences and didn't look carefully at the print. When he reread, he got the first part of the sentence but used the word "stove" instead of "oven," which was not familiar to him. Stanley didn't try to use the first letter of "oven," as he often does, because the vowel sound at the beginning was unlikely to help Malcolm.

Supporting beginning readers as they tackle new materials is a challenging task for tutors. Stanley is an experienced tutor and has learned some appropriate responses. Over time, you, too, will become better at intervening during reading. Set yourself the challenge of developing a repertoire of responses that you can draw on to help your child. Figure 4.15 is a list you might want to photocopy and keep available for reference as you are learning.

Sometimes, you will find that your child needs more than occasional support on the first reading of a book. If the book is too difficult, you might say, "Let's read this together," and proceed with a *choral reading* of the book, or ask your child to repeat a sentence after you read it using a technique called *echo reading*. Use these forms of support only until the child can go it alone. With choral reading, you can often fade out or hold back while the child begins to take the lead. Like the role of a parent teaching a child to ride a bike, the tutor must be prepared to provide support when the child is teetering and to let go when the child is steady. But remember, if a child continues to miss more than two or three words on the second reading, you may have chosen a book that is just too difficult. If this happens, be ready to take the responsibility by saying something like "I didn't choose that book very well. I'll find you another one."

After the First Reading of a New Book

There are several things you should do after your child completes the new book. First of all, offer some positive feedback in a sincere and specific way:

"You read that very well. There was only one word that tripped you up, and you figured it out by looking at the picture."

"That book had a couple of difficult spots, but you worked very hard to figure out those new words."

"I like the way you . . . used expression, went back to fix a word, looked for clues, and so on."

Next, talk about the book a bit in a conversational way. You can model your own reactions with comments such as "Boy, that book makes me feel hungry" or "I would have liked some more things on my pizza." Get your child to express her own reactions with questions such as "Did you like that book?"; "What did you like about it?"; "Would you want to . . . ?" Do not grill your child with questions such as "What did he put on the pizza first?" or "Who helped him make a pizza?" A good book preview ensures that your child will be reading for meaning and the simple books read at this level do not present comprehension problems. However, if you think your child might not understand something, don't hesitate to talk about it or to look at the illustrations again. Remember, in these simple books, much of the story is told through the

FIGURE 14.15.

Intervening with Your Child during Reading

Remember that the most important thing to do is WAIT.
Give your child time to discover and correct a problem.

When your child gets off track, say:

"Point to each word as you read."

"Try that again and touch each word."

When your child substitutes a wrong word, say:

"Does that make sense? Try it again."

"Does that sound right? Try it again."

"Let's look at this word again. What letter do you see at the beginning?"

"Try using this sound to say the word." *(Point to the first letter.)*

"Could this word be *(repeat the error)*? Why not?"

"What else could you try there?"

"_____ makes sense, but look at the first letter."

"You've almost got it, try again."

When your child comes to a word and just stops, say:

"What can you do to figure out that word?"

"Does the picture help?"

"What would make sense. Read it again."

"Could that word be *(use the correct word)*? Try it and see if it works."

"Is there a part of that word you can read?"

When your child makes a correction, say:

"Were you right?"

"I like the way you fixed that."

"How did you know that word was _____ ?"

"You figured that out yourself."

"Good work getting that right."

"You got it. Read it again."

Sometimes the best thing you can do is just give the word.

pictures. After some brief informal conversation, ask your child to read the book again.

Children will nearly always read better the second time through, having mastered many of the problems the first time. This second reading will make the child feel more successful, and the reading will be more pleasurable. The second reading will also increase the familiarity of the book, so that when you return to it several days or a week later, the child will have a good chance of being successful.

When Malcolm reread *My Pizza*, he paused at the word "oven," not knowing what to say. Stanley concluded that this was probably a new vocabulary word, and that he might just have to supply it for a while. Malcolm breezed through the rest of the book. Stanley shook his hand, saying, "You did a great job that time. We'll keep working on that word 'oven'." Malcolm beamed and left the session that day feeling very good about himself.

Further Reading of the New Book

Put the new book in the collection of books for rereading at the next tutoring session. In some situations, you may be able to send the new book or other books back to the class or home for the child to practice, but this depends upon the way your program is organized and the resources you have. The little books used by emergent readers are thin and seem to get lost easily. If you do send books home, it is probably best to place the book in a 9 × 11 manila envelope with the child's name on it.

Using Rhymes, Jingles, and Poetry

Poems and jingles also make appropriate reading materials, but you will need to introduce them in a different way, because they seldom have much support from pictures and may have many unfamiliar words. Poems are meant to be heard in order to enjoy the rhythm, colorful language, and imagery. Children may enjoy poems more if they can hear them read first by an expert reader. Begin with an introduction that stimulates interest, and briefly summarizes what the poem is about. Read the poem or jingle to your child once or twice as your child listens. Invite the child on the third reading to *choral read* along with you as you point to the words. Be ready to fade out if you sense that your child can take the lead. Fall back on *echo reading* (in which the child repeats a line after you) if there is a part that seems to be especially difficult.

Poems and jingles are good reading material and are fun to reread, but they are not leveled. You will need to use your judgment about how appropriate they are in terms of difficulty. If your child still cannot read a poem after choral reading several times, it may be too hard.

Looking Ahead

This lesson plan is appropriate for any emergent reader who cannot read at the primer level, as described in Chapter 3. If the child you are working with can read at the primer level, either initially or after you have worked with him or her for a while, use the early reader plan described in the next chapter.

Observation Guide for the New Reading Materials Introduction

Ask yourself the following questions to assess how well your student did with a new book. Record your observations on the lesson plan in the comments section.

- How successful was your child's effort to read the first time?
- What kinds of errors did your child make, and how did you intervene?
- What changes might you make in your book previews?
- How well did your child do on the second reading of the book?
- Was the book a good choice in terms of the level of difficulty?
- Did your child seem to enjoy and understand the book?
- What did your child have to say about the book after reading it?

Evaluating Yourself as a Tutor on the New Book Introduction

After completing several new book introductions, you might check yourself on the following points:

- Did I read the title to my child and talk about the picture on the cover?
- Before reading, did I ask my child what she thought the book might be about?
- Before reading, did we look at the illustrations inside the book and comment on what we saw?
- Am I learning to anticipate the problems my child might make on a first reading?
- Is my child able to read the first time, with only a few interventions from me?
- Am I giving my child time to discover her own errors and attempt to correct them?
- Am I developing a repertoire of intervention responses?
- After reading, am I revisiting problem words or pages before reading again?
- Am I giving my child positive feedback on her efforts?
- Am I sharing my own responses to the book and asking my child for hers?

Reference

Blachman, B.A., Ball, E., Black, S., & Tangle, O. (1994). Kindergarten teachers develop phonemic awareness in low-income, inter-city classrooms: Does it make a difference? *Reading and Writing: An Interdisciplinary Journal, 6,* 1–17.

CHAPTER 5

General Tutoring Plan for the Early Reader

Early readers are distinguished from emergent readers by their ability to read early- to middle-first-grade material independently. Early readers can recognize many words out of context and score at least 80% (16 words correct) on the preprimer word list. They will probably know at least 50% of the words on the primer list and the first-grade list as well. They should be able to read *Sam* and *My Huge Dog Max* to criterion, and they may be able to read a primer-level passage. If your child could read 90–100% of the words on the first-grade list, he or she is beyond the early reader category, but you will still find the lesson plan outlined in this chapter helpful. Early readers can represent and use beginning, middle, and ending sounds in their spelling and reading. They are generally ready for a review of short vowels and lots of work on long vowel patterns.

The early reader lesson plan was developed for those children who are still behind their grade-level peers, but who have outgrown the simple, predictable materials used with emergent readers. The early reader plan is sometimes used for first graders in the latter part of the year, for second graders, or for any reader at any grade who is reading at the primer to second-grade level. This plan focuses more upon comprehension and does not include the word bank described for the emergent reader. Early readers still need to study words and increase the store of sight words they recognize automatically, but they acquire new words more readily, and a collection of known words on cards would become too large and unwieldy. In this chapter, you will meet Charla, a second grader, and her tutor Phyllis. They have been working together for several months, and Charla is now reading at a Primer level.

Overview of the Early Reader Plan

The lesson plan for the early reader consists of three main parts:

1. *Reading for fluency* (5–10 minutes): During this warm-up and practice, children read aloud easy materials and reread familiar materials to enhance their speed, expression, and accuracy.

2. *Reading and writing* (20–30 minutes): In this part of the plan, children read materials at their instructional level and engage in comprehension activities.

3. *Word study and phonics* (5–10 minutes): During this time, children examine and compare words to help them develop understandings and generalizations about how letters represent sounds.

A fourth part can often be added when time allows:

4. *Revisiting favorite reading materials or more writing* (5 minutes)

A sample lesson plan can be seen in Figure 5.1, and a blank form, which may be copied for your use, can be found in Appendix A, page 130. You will see that there is a space for you to write in comments to describe how well your child accomplished the various tasks. These comments will serve as guides for future planning and provide important documentation of your child's progress. After each section of the plan described below, there are questions to guide your observations and to assess your own tutoring skills.

Early Reader Lesson Plan
Part I: Reading for Fluency

Every early reader tutoring session begins with the oral reading of easy material or the rereading of familiar material to develop children's reading fluency. Until children can read fluently, with a high degree of accuracy, smoothness, and good speed, reading will feel like hard work. When children read easy materials, they feel successful and enjoy the experience of reading for fun. Reading easy and familiar materials serves as a warm-up, helps children grow as they gain more familiarity with words, and develops a feeling of competence, mastery, and control.

Reading for Fluency includes one of the following: (1) the reading of easy books, (2) *timed repeated readings*, (3) poetry reading , and (4) the oral rereading of something read during the last session. This part of the plan should last about 5–10 minutes.

Materials to Use to Develop Fluency

Easy material for early readers includes poetry, simple books, and short stories that they can read with 95% accuracy or better, or no more than one error in every 15–20 words. More challenging materials at the child's instructional level will be read during the Reading and Writing portion of the plan.

FIGURE 5.1. Sample lesson plan, full size.

Early Plan Student __Charla__   Tutor __Phyllis__   Date __April 14__   Lesson # __32__

Lesson Plan	Description of Planned Activities	Time	Outcomes and Comments
Rereading or Easy Reading	Books: Reread Rainy Day Poema her choice Timed Repeated Reading: My Yellow Cat p. 5-9	10	Used word parts to f... out "track." Review word family fa—ack with Blanda next week. Find Cat poems. TRR: 29 wpm, 41 wpm, 45 wpm
Reading and Writing	Book: Cookie Week Level: 10 Preview: Talk about title and look at first few pictures. Read first 4 pages. Written Response Question: What will happen next? Second Response Question: What did you like best about their story? Read again if time	20	Loved the book! Might try writing one like it. Used word parts to get "upset." Couldn't get "everywhere" 1st time but did on reading. Self correcting better. Wrote Cookie will git in mor trubl for prediction and trubl. Cookie fell in the toylt and made a mes. Corrected the vowel in "mess" to an e when reminded. Remembered her periods!
Word Study	1. Picture/Word Sort: Sort short A, E, and O 3. Writing Sort: Write 3 words for each vowel 4. Word Hunt: Look for short vowel words in new book.	15	Read and sorted words quickly. Misspelled "step" as STAP. Looked for short O words in Cookie Week. Found: on, got, pots, and closet. Revisit next time for short E.
Revisit Book or Writing	Reread My Yellow Cat and time it again.	—	No extra time today.

Charla worked hard today!

There are a number of different things you might invite your child to read during this time, and early readers benefit from practicing their reading in a variety of formats. Have a collection of materials, so that you can offer your child a choice.

1. *Books at an easier level:* The materials used for easy reading might include some of the same books used for the emergent reader. Whereas the emergent reader could read these books only with your support, the early reader can read these books independently. Books that the child particularly enjoys might be read several times over several sessions. Others may be read only once. Start by looking for books between Levels 7 and 9, which are listed in Appendix B, or books that have been purchased and leveled as described in Chapter 2. Adjust these levels as you observe your child's success. If books at a particular level seem too easy or fail to interest your child, try higher level books. Go back to easier levels if your child cannot read nearly every word on his or her own.

2. *Poetry:* Reading poetry provides an excellent opportunity to practice expressive, fluent reading. Since poetry is meant to be read aloud, it is a particularly appropriate medium for oral reading practice. Eloise Greenfield, Karla Kuskin, Jack Prelutsky, Lee Bennett Hopkins, Shel Silverstein, Kalli Dakos, and many others write or collect delightful poetry for children. Children especially enjoy humorous poems, but avoid poems with lots of multisyllabic words or tongue twisters. Read a selected poem to your child in your best oral reading style. Invite your child to read *chorally* along with you a second time before tackling it independently. Troublesome lines can be practiced with echo reading (in echo reading, the child repeats a portion of the text right after you read it to her). Favorite poems can be photocopied or typed and put into a collection the child can reread many times and eventually take home. Some children like to hear themselves read poetry on a tape recorder, and this can serve as an added incentive for practicing.

3. *Familiar materials:* The most convenient source of easy reading material will be material that has been read before. The classroom teacher or a resource teacher who works with the student might send materials from time to time that the child has been reading. Also, encourage the child to reread a book or a portion of a book that he enjoyed and read successfully in the last tutoring session. This might also be used for a timed repeated reading, described below.

Timed Repeated Readings

Timed repeated reading (TRR) provides tangible evidence of progress in reading speed and accuracy, and many children respond well to this activity. Try TRR with your child and use it regularly, if not every session. The child reads aloud an easy passage of around 100 words several times, while the tutor keeps track of the time and the number of errors. Always time children's first or second reading as a baseline. This way, you can nearly always be sure they will improve after a third or fourth reading. You will need a stopwatch or a clock with a second hand. A calculator may come in handy as well. There are three ways to do a TRR:

1. *Timed reading:* The easiest way is to count the number of seconds it takes to read the same passage. This number should get smaller after each rereading.

2. *One-minute reading:* A second easy way is to simply have your child read for 1 minute and count up the number of words she read each time. This number should get bigger after each rereading.

3. *Words per minute:* The third way is actually to calculate words per minute. You will need to count the number of words in a selected book or passage before timing the reading. Words per minute are calculated by multiplying the number of words in the passage times 60, and then dividing by the number of seconds it took the child to read it. For example, Charla read a 64-word passage in 2 minutes and 14 seconds (or 134 seconds):

$$\frac{64 \text{ words} \times 60 \text{ seconds}}{134 \text{ (time spent reading in seconds)}} = 29 \text{ words per minute}$$

Charla was able to improve this reading rate to 45 words per minute after two more readings, and to 50 words per minute in another session. Whichever way you choose to conduct your TRR, it is important that your child see tangible evidence of her progress. This can be in the form of a bar or line graph. An example of a TRR graph for words per minute is shown in Figure 5.2 and forms are available in Appendix A, page 145. Circle "words," "seconds," or "WPM" on the form to indicate what you are counting and recording on the graph.

FIGURE 5.2. Timed repeated reading chart.

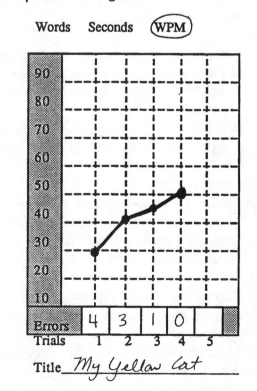

Errors during Timed Repeated Readings

Keep track of the number of errors the child makes during a TRR and record these as well. The number of errors should decrease over several readings. When your child makes an error during a TRR, do not correct it at the time, but revisit it after the reading. If a child pauses and needs your help, simply supply the word but, again, revisit it. To revisit a word after the timed reading, ask the child to read again the sentence in which the error occurred.

Responding to Errors during Reading for Fluency

First of all remember that children should not be making more than one error in 15–20 words. If they are, you should find something easier to read. Do not interrupt or engage children in lengthy discussions about what a word might be during a timed reading, but do be ready to respond to an error or an appeal for help when they are simply reading. How you respond will depend upon a number of factors. A word that does not change the meaning of the book or story might just be ignored. For example, Charla substituted the word "home" for "house" in the sentence "Mr. Zumo painted his *house* red and yellow." Phyllis decided not to interrupt Charla to correct the error, since it made perfectly good sense either way. She could come back and revisit the word "house" when Charla was done reading. If she had substituted "horse" for "house," it would not have made sense, and Phyllis would intervene immediately:

> "Did that make sense to you? Let's try it again."
>
> "Look at this word again."
>
> "What else could that word be?"

Early readers have more knowledge of phonics and may be able to use word parts to figure out unfamiliar words. Read how Phyllis helps Charla with the word "track " in the sentence "Don't track in mud":

> Charla: Don't . . . *(She pauses, stuck on the word "track.")*
> Phyllis: *(She waits for 5 seconds.)* Look at that word carefully. Do you see a part that you can read?
> Charla: tr . . . ack.
> Phyllis: See if that works. *(Charla starts over and gets the sentence right.)* We have done a sort with -ACK words, haven't we. *(She makes a note to revisit the -ACK family next session and focus on -ACK words that begin with blends such as "stack," "snack," and "quack.")*

Pages 95 to 97 in Chapter 4 on the emergent reader have other suggestions for offering assistance when children make errors or come to a word they cannot read. You might want to make a copy of the chart on page 97 and keep it handy until you master a variety of responses. If there seem to be no cues you can offer that will help children, or if they are unable to use the cues you suggest, simply say the word.

Observation Guide for the Fluency Part of the Lesson Plan

Ask yourself the following questions to assess how well your child did during the Reading for Fluency part of the plan. Record your observations on the lesson plan as a guide for future planning.

- What did your child read, and what level are the materials?
- Did your child read with interest? What did she particularly enjoy?
- What problems arose, what did you do, and what did the child do?
- If you did a TRR, how much did she improve?
- How much time was spent reading?
- What will you do differently next time?

Evaluating Yourself as a Tutor on the Fluency Part of the Lesson Plan

You can use the following checklist to assess your own tutoring skill:

- Do I have a selection of materials from which the child can choose?
- Do I record the book titles and how many times each is read?
- Do I give my child time to think before offering assistance?
- Do I monitor the amount of time we spend reading (5–10 minutes)?
- Do I use TRRs and keep records of my child's improvement on a chart.
- Do I make notes about what my child does well and what she has trouble with?

Early Reader Lesson Plan
Part II: Reading and Writing

Reading and writing are the heart of the early reader tutorial. New reading material is previewed, and the first few pages are read aloud by the child. Before further reading, the child is asked to write a prediction of what he thinks may happen next, or a summary of what has happened so far. Following this response, the child reads on, with intermittent pauses to discuss further developments. If the child can read at a late first grade level this reading should be done silently. At the story's conclusion, or at the day's stopping point, the child is asked to write a second response. This response consists of an evaluation of the first response, based on the new, just read, information. The child's writing not only enhances his comprehension but also exercises his growing knowledge of spelling and phonics. This part of the lesson should last approximately 20–30 minutes.

Selecting Books for Reading and Writing

Choosing books that the child can read with only an occasional problem is the first critical step in the reading and writing portion of the plan (Figure 3.5). Use the initial assessment and the chart in Figure 3.5 as a rough guide, then note how successful your child is at reading material at particular numbered levels. Be ready to try an easier level if he is missing more than one word in 10. Try a higher level if he can breeze through the material reading quickly, making no more than one error in 20 words or less. At your first tutoring session, take materials at a range of numbered levels (such as 9–12), and have your child read from several levels until you find a good match. Over time, your child should be able to read at higher levels as a sign of progress.

For older early readers, you can capitalize not only on their individual interests, but also on curricular topics that parallel those being covered in the classroom. Children who are poor readers often have great difficulty reading the content-area textbooks used in their classrooms. To help them out, find some books at their level on the topics they are studying.

Presenting New Material for Reading and Writing

New reading material is presented through the following steps:

1. *Preview the material:* The child reads the title and, together with the tutor, examines and discusses the pictures on the cover or the first few pages of the text. The child might be asked what she already knows about the topic, the author, or the type of story.

2. *Begin reading:* The child reads several pages of the story or text. The tutor should support the child's understanding, as needed, by discussing unusual vocabulary and new concepts.

3. *First written response:* The first few pages offer the child some background information on the topic or ideas about the upcoming story line. At this point, the tutor should ask the child to make a prediction:

"What do you think is going to happen next?" (for stories)

"What kind of information do you think the author is going to tell us about next?" (for information books)

If your child has no idea what might happen next, you can ask him to summarize what has happened so far: "What have you found out so far?" After some discussion, the child is expected to write down his prediction or brief summary in one or two sentences.

4. *Continue reading:* As the child continues to read, encourage him to react to new events or information and discuss them in an informal way. Discuss new vocabulary and ideas, but do not grill him with questions that "test" his comprehension. If your child misunderstands something, have him reread the part of the text that will help clear up the confusion.

5. *Second written response:* At the end of the session or the day's stopping point, engage your child in further discussion before asking him to write a second response. This discussion consists of an evaluation of the first response ("Did that turn out the way you thought?") or your and the child's reaction to the story or the new information. Model your own response, such as " I liked the part where . . .," "I didn't know that . . .," or "That story reminds me of. . . ." After some discussion, ask your child to write one or two sentences again.

"What did happen? What might happen next?" (for a story)
"What did you learn?" (for an information book)
"What did you like best about this book?"

6. *Revisit the book:* You might ask your child to reread a favorite portion of the book, or a portion that presented some problems. This is a good point to look back at some of the words that were unfamiliar to your child and read the sentences again where they occurred. This will increase the likelihood that he will remember that word when he sees it again.

Let's see how Phyllis and Charla accomplish the reading and writing part of the plan. Today, she is going to try a Level 10 book entitled *Cookie's Week* by Cindy Ward. The book starts with the two sentences: "On Monday . . . Cookie fell into the toilet. There was water everywhere." Each succeeding pair of sentences repeats the pattern with a different day and a new calamity.

Phyllis: Charla, I found you another book about a cat. The cat is named Cookie. *(Phyllis lays* Cookie's Week *before Charla.)* Can you read the title?
Charla: Cookie . . . *Cookie's Week.*
Phyllis: Good. You noticed that -'s at the end of Cookie. Let's look at the first few pages and see what this book is going to be about. What is happening to Cookie in this picture?
Charla: It looks like she is in the toilet.
Phyllis: Have you ever heard of a cat in the toilet? I wonder what she was doing there.
Charla: Maybe she was trying to get a drink.
Phyllis: That's a good idea. Let's read a few pages.
Charla: *(She starts to read the first page.)* On Monday Cookie fell into the toilet. There was water . . . *(She pauses on the word "everywhere," which she doesn't know.)*
Phyllis: Can you try the sentence again?
Charla: There was water . . .
Phyllis: *(Waits 5 seconds)* Could it be "everywhere"?
Charla: There was water everywhere. *(Charla goes on to read the next two pages successfully, and at this point, Phyllis stops her to write a prediction.)*
Phyllis: What do you think is going to happen in the rest of this story?
Charla: I think Cookie is going to get into more trouble.
Phyllis: Why do you say that?
Charla: Well, on Monday she got in the toilet, and on Tuesday, she knocked over a plant, so on Wednesday, something else like that might happen.
Phyllis: Let's write down what you think will happen. *(Charla writes, "Cookie will git in mor trubl." She copied "Cookie" from the cover and wrote the rest of the words on her own.)* Read your sentence for me. *(Charla reads.)* That's certainly possible. Now let's find out what happens. *(Charla reads on, but pauses at the word "upset." Phyllis gives her time to think before intervening.)* Can you read part of that word? Look at the first two letters.

Charla: Up . . . s . . . et, upset!

Phyllis: Try that and see if it works. *(Charla continues to read, needing Phyllis's help on several more words and figuring out others on her own, but not making more than one mistake in 10 words.)* Were you right about what was going to happen in this story? *(Charla nods.)* Cookie sure did get into a lot of trouble, didn't she. Would you want to have a cat like that around your house?

Charla: I think my Mom would get mad at her and make me clean up all her mess.

Phyllis: I think you are right. Did you like this book?

Charla: Yeah. I liked where she fell in the toilet. That would be really yucky.

Phyllis: Do you want to write about that for your last sentence?

Charla: Okay. *(She writes: Cokie fell in the toylt and made a mas.)*

Phyllis: What do you need to put at the end of your sentence? *(Charla adds a period.)* Let's look at the word "mess" again. *(Charla has been sorting words with short vowels.)* Say it slowly and listen to the vowel in the middle. What other vowel could go there? *(Charla changes the "a" to "e.")* Since *Cookie's Week* wasn't a very long book, I'd like to hear you read it again, right now.

On the second reading, Charla whizzed through the book, with only one or two pauses to reconsider words. Phyllis made a note to look for some more books at Level 10, as well as some more books about cats, which Charla seems to enjoy. Phyllis and Charla discussed the book together and shared reactions in a conversational way. Phyllis intervened with help when she was needed. In one case, she just gave Charla the word, but in another case, Charla was able to look at the pieces of a word and figure it out, based upon her knowledge of other words she knew or by sounding it out.

Using Information Books

Many children enjoy information books and benefit from the knowledge they can gain from reading about dinosaurs, astronauts, sharks, airplanes, and so on. The steps you follow are the same as those described for reading and writing, but the focus will be "What do you want to learn?"; "What will the author tell us?"; and "What did you find out?"; and not upon making predictions such as "What do you think will happen?" You may want to have your child do the writing in a "fact book" on a particular subject that can be added to over several sessions. By dividing the paper into columns labeled, for example "Where they live" and "What they eat," your child can take notes as he reads several books about wild animals.

Mammals

Name	Live	Eeat	Enimes	Babes
Blak Bare Bear	Woods	roots bares	man	cubs
Kiler Wales	Osun	Seels fish	man	Caf
Frut	rain	frute	?	baby

Questions Tutors Often Ask

What Do I Do When My Child Makes a Mistake or Turns to Me for Help while Reading?

You can expect your child to make errors and encounter words that she does not know when she is reading new materials, as Charla did above. These problems are really opportunities to grow and should be left up to her to solve as much as possible. If you just supply the missing or miscalled word every time, your child will grow dependent on you instead of learning how to handle problems independently. The first thing you do when your child needs help is to *do nothing*. Stop and think, and give the child time to think as well. See if you can determine the source of the problem and think of questions you can ask to guide your child to solve the problem. An often-used response to an error is simply "Try that again." Sometimes, you may choose to ignore an error if it does not change the meaning of the sentence, and sometimes, there may be nothing better to do than just tell your child what it is. As a reading tutor, your skill in making decisions about how to intervene appropriately is important and will grow with experience. Refer to pages 95 to 97 in Chapter 4 for a fuller discussion of errors and your response to them.

How Accurate Does Children's Spelling Need to Be When They Write?

In general, accept your child's spelling efforts but hold him accountable for what he has been taught during the word study portion of your lessons, as Phyllis did with Charla on the word "mess." You might remind your child of similar words that he knows how to spell. For example, if he spells "bike" as BIK, you could remind him that "bike" is spelled the same way as "like," a word many early readers know. Your child's efforts on the spelling assessment and your ongoing word study will serve as a guide to what you can expect your child to handle when he writes.

There are some words you may want to spell for your child: common words such as "said," "they," "could," and so on. These *high-frequency* words show up often in reading materials and are needed when we write; however, they are hard to sound out and spell phonetically. You may want to write the word for your child to copy or correct on his own paper, but don't overdo this. One or two in a sentence are enough. Too much emphasis on correct spelling may discourage your child from writing.

What about Other Conventions such as Punctuation and Capitalization?

Remind your child about common conventions such as capitals, space between words, and ending punctuation, but, again, don't overdo it. The writing your child does during this part of the plan will not be reread and need not be perfect. It is okay to let some things slide, especially since your time is better spent on reading than editing.

What If My Child Refuses to Write?

Writing is hard work, and many children are reluctant to write, especially those who also find reading difficult. Deemphasizing spelling and writing conventions will be important for reluctant writers until they develop some confidence. Encourage your child to spell "as best she can." Getting one's idea firmly in place before trying to write it down may be helpful too. Ask your child to tell you what it is she wants to write, and be ready to repeat it for her as she starts to write the sentence. You might want to jot down some key words to refer to as she writes. Sometimes, a special pencil, pen, paper, or notebook that is only used during writing can provide an incentive.

What If My Child Is Reluctant to Write Predictions?

When volunteers first begin tutoring an early reader, it is important for them to model "think-alouds," or the process of thinking out loud. For example, if a child cannot come up with a prediction, the tutor might make a prediction "out loud," then tell the child how he came up with it. The tutor might say, "Hmm, it looks like the dog is digging a hole under the fence. . . . I think he might be trying to escape. I think this story might be about his adventure when he gets out. What do you think?"

If the child is reluctant to write down his predictions, you can model the process by writing your own predictions on your own sheet of paper. You might make a game of this, hiding your own prediction until your child has written his. You can then compare predictions. You and your child can both read on to see whose prediction was closest. It is important that your child see you as a partner in this reading/writing process. While he reads, you read. While he writes, you write. By engaging in the process along with your child, you will elevate reading to a shared intellectual pursuit, and you will not be viewed as a task master.

Observation Guide for Reading and Writing

Ask yourself the following questions about the reading and writing portion of the plan and record your observations on the lesson plan in the comments section:

- How successfully is your child able to read the material you present?
- Is your child able to make predictions and write brief summaries?
- What kind of problems occur as your child reads, and how do you and your child handle them?
- How willing is your child to write?
- Is he able to represent in his writing the sounds that you expect?
- What help does he require from you?
- How well does your child do with the conventions of writing, such as letter formation, spaces, capitals, punctuation, and so on?

Evaluating Yourself as a Tutor on Reading and Writing

After completing this portion of the plan, you might check yourself on the following points:

- Do I have reading material ready that I think my child will enjoy reading with success?

- Do I intervene only after giving my child time to solve a problem on her own?

- Do I have a repertoire of suggestions that I can use to intervene appropriately?

- Do I discuss the reading material in a conversational way, offering and encouraging personal reactions and comments?

- Do I let my child do the writing and lend support only as needed?

- Do I offer simple tips and suggestions about writing conventions when appropriate, but am I also willing to let some things "slide"?

- Do I have reasonable expectations about what my child can spell based upon the information I have from the assessment and from our progress in word study?

Early Reader Lesson Plan
Part III: Word Study for Phonics

The word study component of the early tutoring plan is divided into three parts: (1) picture and word sorting, (2) writing sorts, and (3) word hunts. *Word sorts* refer to the categorization of known words according to contrasting phonics features. For example, short-A words such as "tap," "fast," "flat," or "sand" are sorted into one category, while short-I words such as "fish," "sit," "thin," and "flip" are sorted into another. After the child sorts these words and describes how the words in each category are alike, he writes the words as you call them out in a notebook. This is the *writing sort*. For the *word hunt*, the child looks through familiar reading material for words with the same features. These words are added to the word study notebook. The word study component of the lesson should last about 10 minutes.

In this part of the plan, you will be encountering terms such as "blends," "short vowels," and so forth. These terms are described in the text with examples, and you can refer to the glossary in the back of the book. An important discussion of vowels is included below.

Planning Word Study and Phonics for the Early Reader

Early readers will have mastered beginning and ending single *consonants* such as the "s" and "t" in "sat." They may still make some mistakes on *consonant blends* (such as the first two consonants in *"blend," "stop,"* and *"train"*), and *short vowels* (as in "bat," "red," and "hop"). A few of the more advanced early readers may have short vowels under pretty good control but leave out or confuse the silent letters that accompany *long vowels* (as in "road," "like," and "ape"). The general sequence for phonics instruction for the early reader is listed below:

Sequence of Early Reader Phonics Instruction	1. Review of consonant blends. 2. Review of word families that have mixed vowels. 3. Compare short vowel sounds in nonrhyming words. Include words with blends and *digraphs* ("that," "chin," "ship," "when"). 4. Compare long vowel sounds to short vowels sounds. 5. Compare long vowel *patterns* to short vowel patterns and to each other.

Where you will start in this sequence depends upon your child's spelling efforts. Refer to Figure 3.6 in Chapter 3. If your child is using short vowels in her spelling but representing them incorrectly, you should review word families with mixed short vowels and then compare short vowel sounds in nonrhyming words. Chapter 4 provides information about activities and word lists that you will need. If your child used but confused the silent letters in words with long vowels (such as spelling "float" as FLOTE or "treat" as TREET), then she is ready for work on long vowel patterns compared with short vowels. The study of long vowel patterns includes a review of short vowels if your child has only occasional problems with those.

Some Background Information on Vowels

The vowels are "a," "e," "i," "o," "u," and sometimes "y." Each of these letters has two basic sounds, long and short. Short vowel sounds are challenging for many young readers, because they do not sound like the name of the letter, as do long vowels. Say the words in the chart below to compare the short vowel sound and the long vowel sound commonly known as:

Vowel	Short vowel sound	Long vowel sound
A	cat	cake
E	pet	feet
I	fix	kite
O	not	coat
U	rug	cute

Many children have difficulty hearing the difference between some of the short vowel sounds. Short "e" and short "i" are very similar in some words, and regional dialects may make this difference even less. In central Virginia, the words "pen" and "pin" are said exactly the same. "Get" often rhymes with "it." The short "o" in "dog" sounds more like "dawg" in many dialects. Listen carefully as your child pronounces words and sorts them. It is a good idea to include a miscellaneous category when sorting to accommodate words that don't quite match the featured vowel sounds. But don't try to correct your child's dialect. We all speak a dialect, and we learn to read and spell by matching our dialect to the spelling patterns that represent it.

Long vowels are easier for children to hear, because the vowel "says its name." The hard part about long vowels is the silent letters that accompany them. Each long vowel sound is spelled with different combinations or *patterns*. For example, the long-"i" sound can be spelled with IE in "pie," I_E as in "kite," IGH as in "light," and Y as in "my." The study of long vowel patterns can extend a long time for most early readers, because there are several patterns for each long vowel sound.

Long and short vowel sounds are the most common vowel sounds, but there are others, such as the sound in "car" or "call," which is neither long nor short. Some are known as "r"-controlled vowels (as in "car") or "l"-controlled (as in "call") . Additional vowel sounds are spelled with OU as in "loud," or OI as in "boil," and there are many more. The study of all these vowels can get quite complex and is beyond the scope of this guidebook. For additional information on word study for vowel patterns, see the book *Words Their Way: Word Study for Phonics, Spelling, and Vocabulary Development* (1996) by D. Bear, M. Invernizzi, S. Templeton, and F. Johnston, published by Merrill/Prentice Hall.

Teaching the Short Vowel Sounds

Below is a suggested sequence for contrasting the short vowel words and pictures. Start with short "a," since it is confused the least. The particular sequence isn't very important, but short "a" and short "e," and short "e" and short "i," are the toughest contrasts and should be dealt with at the end.

Sequence for Short Vowel Contrasts	1. Compare short "a" with short "i" (these sounds are fairly distinct; compare item 2).
	2. Compare short "o" with short "a" (add a new sound to one already studied).
	3. Compare short "i," short "o," and short "a" (try three categories to review).
	4. Compare short "e" and short "u" (compare two more).
	5. Compare all short vowels in various combinations ("a," "e," "i," "o," "u").

Picture Sorts for Short Vowels.   Use pictures of words spelled with short vowels for picture sorts followed by writing sorts, as described in the previous chapter. The following steps use the pictured sort as an example (see Figure 5.3).

1. You will need pictures of words spelled with the short vowels (for example, short "a" and short "i"). Use a letter to head each category.

2. Model the sort by placing a picture (such as a picture of a "hat") under the card with the middle vowel letter ("a") and break the word into sounds by peeling off the beginning consonant and then the ending consonant (say something like "hat, at, a—this sound is called short "a.")

FIGURE 5.3.   Picture sort of short vowels "a" and "i."

3. Repeat this with a picture for each sound (for example, "fish," "fish, ish, i—this sound is a short 'i'").

4. Model several more picture sorts and then hand the pictures to your child. You can let him sort from then on or take turns sorting.

5. If your child makes a mistake, ask him to try peeling off the beginning and ending sounds as shown earlier and help him sort the vowel into the correct category.

6. After sorting, ask you child to name all of the pictures in a category and tell you how they are all alike (for example, "They all have the same vowel sound in the middle").

7. Ask your child to sort all of the pictures again on his own, leaving any mistakes to be found at the end, when the pictures in each category are said aloud.

Basic Procedure for Word Sorts with Short Vowels.   You can find a list of words spelled with short vowels in the word family list in Appendix A (page 140), as well as the lists in this chapter on pages 119–120. The suggested sequence may be altered depending upon how easily and successfully your child can master the short vowels. A brief review might compare three or four short vowels at a time for only a few sessions. A child who needs more help might compare two or three vowels over many weeks. The basic procedure is described below and refers to the sample sort in Figure 5.4.

1. Prepare a collection of words that the child can read. Write the words on small cards or use the template in Appendix A, which can be copied, filled in with words, and cut apart for sorting.

2. Use a letter, picture, or word to use as a column header for each category and lay it down to start the sort (for example, "cat," "sit," and "hot," as used earlier). Model how to isolate the vowel in each word by "peeling off" the first sound and then the last, leaving only the vowel sound in the middle ("cat," "at," "a").

FIGURE 5.4. Word sort with short "a," "i," and "o" with miscellaneous catagory.

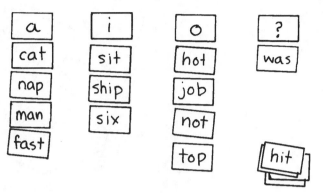

3. Shuffle the rest of the words and turn over one. Read the word and put it under the correct header by vowel sound. Isolate the vowel as described in Step 2. Repeat with several words.

4. Ask the child to do the next word. She should read the new word and sort it under the correct header. If she should hesitate or make a mistake, model how to isolate the vowel and ask her to repeat it. Then, see that the word goes into the correct category on this first sort. The column headed by a question mark is the miscellaneous category, where children may put words they aren't sure of.

5. After all the words have been sorted, ask your child to read down from the top and listen for the vowel sound in each word. Ask your child how the words in each column are alike. In the case of the earlier sort, you want her to notice that the words under "cat" all have an A in the middle. Explain that the sound in the middle of the words is called "short A."

6. Ask your child to sort the words again on her own. Leave errors to be corrected at the end by asking the child to check each row. If your child doesn't find an error, say something like "One of these words is in the wrong place. Can you find it?"

Writing Sort for Short Vowels.   Immediately after your child has sorted words into categories you need to move to the writing sort described here. This will assure that children are not simply sorting by the spelling they *see* but can also *hear* the sound associated with the letters. A sample from a word study notebook with "a," "i," and "o" categories is shown in Figure 5.5.

1. Ask your child to write a header for each category by writing a key word or letter at the top of each column. This can be done in a word study notebook.

2. Call out three or more words for each category in a scrambled order for the child to spell. If you call out "mad," she should write it under the word "cat." Assist your child when needed by saying the word slowly, drawing out the sounds and stressing each one: "mmm-aaa-d." Ask your child to

FIGURE 5.5. Writing sort for short "a," "i," and "o," with word hunt additions.

say each word slowly too. You can expect the child to spell the entire word correctly.

3. As soon as she has written the word, show her the word card for her to self-check. If an error is made, simply ask her to draw a line through it (no need to erase) and write it again in the correct column.

Word Hunt for Short Vowels.   Word hunts will help children extend their understanding of vowel spellings to reading. By finding new words with the same vowel sounds, children learn to apply their knowledge of how short vowels are spelled to decoding new words in text. Children can hunt through books, stories, or poems that they have already read to find additional words with the same sounds. These words should be added to the writing sort in the word study notebook (see Figure 5.5). Many words may turn up in word hunts that appear to fit the pattern but don't fit the sound, or vice versa. For example, your child may find "was" and "car" in his reading material and be ready to write them under "cat," simply because they have an "a" in the middle. These words may look like they fit, but they don't have the right vowel sound. Words that cannot be categorized should be listed in a miscellaneous column of the word study notebook, as shown in the example, which shows a writing sort followed by word hunt entries.

Teaching the Long Vowel Sounds

The study of long vowel patterns described below is appropriate for your child and will serve as a review of short vowels as well. Short vowel words are included as a contrast in the first long vowel sorts. For example, your child's first introduction to long "a" might be in the form of a sort like the one in Figure 5.6.

Additional sorts will contrast other long and short vowels as well as compare different spelling patterns for a particular long vowel sound. The suggested sequence of vowel study listed below should cover the needs of children in the early reader stage. The word study for long vowels occurs at two levels: (1) sorting by sound, and (2) sorting by pattern.

FIGURE 5.6. Word sort for short and long "a."

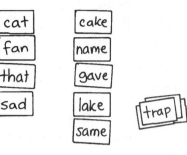

<table>
<tr><td>

Suggested Sequence of Comparisons for Short and Long Vowel Study

</td><td>

1. **A-Sort by Sound:**
   Short "a" (bad, bag, bat, can, cat, dad, had, has, hat, man, pan, pat, ran, sad, sat, that, than, back, fast, last, track, path)

   Long "a" spelled with silent "e" (ate, bake, cake, came, cave, face, gave, lake, made, make, place, same, take, name)

   A-Sort by Sound and Pattern:
   Short "a" and *long "a" spelled with silent "e"* as listed above but add two other patterns

   Long "a" spelled with AI (paint, rain, tail, train, mail, nail, pail, sail, wait)

   Long "a" spelled with AY (day, jay, may, play, say, stay, way, pay, gray)

2. **E-Sort by Sound:**
   Short "e" (bed, leg, pet, red, wet, yes, ten, get, when, hen, web, shed, yet, best, fell, help, tell, well, went, yell, egg, nest)

   Long "e" spelled with two "e's" (bee, feed, feel, green, keep, need, see, seed, seen, sheep, sleep, three, tree, meet, week, queen, sweet)

   E-Sort by Sound and Pattern:
   Short "e" and *long "e" with two "e's"* as listed above but add another pattern

   Long "e" spelled with EA (bean, clean, each, eat, mean, real, sea, seat, teach)

3. **I-Sort by Sound:**
   Short "i" (big, bit, chin, did, fix, hid, him, his, if, lip, mix, pig, sit, six, swim, this, trip, win, zip, dig, hit, kid, ship, fill, fish, hill, miss, pick, wish)

   Long "i" spelled with silent "e" (bike, bite, dime, fine, hide, kite, like, line, nice, ride, side, smile, time, white, drive, five, ice, mice, nine)

   I-Sort by Sound and Pattern:
   Short "i" and *long "i" spelled with silent "e"* as listed above but add two others

   Long "i" with IGH (high, light, might, night, right, fight, right, sigh, sight)

   Long "i" with Y (cry, fly, my, sky, try, why, by, dry, shy)

</td></tr>
</table>

4. **O-Sort by Sound:**

    Short "o" (box, drop, fox, got, hop, hot, lot, mom, mop, not, pot, shop, stop, top, dot, job, lock, rock, sock)

    Long "o" spelled with silent "e" (bone, close, drove, hole, nose, note, rope, stone, those, rope, joke, rode, rose, smoke)

    O-Sort by Sound and Pattern:

    Short "o" and *long "o" with silent "e"* as listed above but add two other patterns

    Long "o" spelled OA (boat, coat, goat, float, road, soap, toad, toast)

    Long "o" spelled with OW (grow, know, show, slow, snow, blow, own)

5. **U-Sort by Sound and Pattern:**

    Short "u" (bus, but, cut, fun, run, sun, up, us, bug, cup, drum, hug, mud, nut, duck, jump, just, must, truck, shut)

    Long "u" with silent "e" (blue, clue, glue, true, cute, use, huge, cube, mule)

    Long "u" with EW (new, grew, chew, drew, few, flew, knew, threw)

Picture Sorts for Long Vowel Sounds.   Begin by sorting pictures by vowel sounds in a manner similar to that described above for short vowels. Lay out about 15 picture cards with a mixture of long and short vowel sounds for a particular letter. Choose a letter as a header for each sound and model several words before turning the task over to your child. In order to isolate the vowel sound, the tutor may model the segmentation process by saying "cake—ake—a, this is the long-'a' sound."

Move to word sorts so that your child can see how long vowels are spelled. Most words with a long vowel sound have a silent letter or letters that signal the long vowel sound. Only after word sorts can you expect your child to spell long vowel words correctly.

Basic Word Sort for Comparing Long and Short Vowel Sounds.

1. Prepare a collection of words that the child can already read. Some suggested words are listed on previous pages, and you can use words your child has seen in the materials you read. Write the words on small cards or the template on page 144, which can be filled in and cut apart for sorting.

2. Select a word to use as a header for each category, and lay it down to start the sort (for example, "cat" and "make") as in Figure 5.6. Model how to isolate the vowel in each word by "peeling off" the first sound and then the last, leaving only the vowel sound in the middle ("cat," "at," "a," and "make," "ake," "a").

3. Shuffle the rest of the words and turn over one. Read the word and put it under the correct header by vowel sound. Isolate the vowel as described in Step 2. Repeat with several words.

4. Ask the child to do the next word. He should read the new word and sort it under the correct header. If he should hesitate or make a mistake, model how to isolate the vowel, and see that it goes into the correct category on this sort.

5. After all the words have been sorted, ask the child to read down from the top and listen for the vowel sound in each word. Ask the child how the words in each column are alike. In the case of the sort above, you want him to notice that the words under "make" all have an "a" in the middle and an "e" at the end, while the words under "cat" have only one vowel in the middle.

6. Ask your child to sort the words again on his own. Leave errors to be corrected at the end, when you ask the child to read down each column to check the words. If a child overlooks a mistake say something like "There is a word in this column that needs to be moved. Let's read down the column and see if we can find it."

Writing Sort for Long and Short Vowels.   Asking your child to write these words into categories will further enforce the patterns that spell the long vowel sounds. These written sorts are recorded in a word study notebook or on a piece of paper.

1. Ask your child to set up the headers (such as "cat" and "make") for the categories you will need by writing them at the top of the paper.

2. Call out three or more words for each category in a mixed fashion for the child to spell, saying the word slowly, if needed. If you call out "mad," the child should write it under the word "cat." You can expect the child to spell the entire word correctly. You can also lay out pictures that correspond to the sounds you have been sorting and let the child select words to write into the correct categories.

3. As soon as she has written the word, show her the word card for her to self-check. If an error is made, simply ask the child to draw a line through it (no need to erase) and write it again in the correct column.

Word Hunt for Long and Short Vowels.   Word hunts extend the application of phonics principles to other words in text. Children learn that many more words have the same vowel sounds and spelling patterns as they hunt through books, stories, or poems that they have already read to find additional words. The words should be added to the writing sort in the word study notebook. Many words may turn up in word hunts that appear to fit the pattern but don't fit the sound, or vice versa. For example, your child may find "have" and "are" in his reading material and be ready to write them under "make." These words have the right pattern (they have an "a" with an "e" at the end) but not the long

sound of "a." Words that cannot be categorized should be listed in a miscellaneous column of the word study notebook.

Basic Two-Step Pattern Sort for Long Vowels Patterns.   This sort differs
slightly from the procedure described on page 120. It begins with a two-step
sort. Words are first sorted by sound, and then they are sorted by spelling patterns (see words listed by patterns on previous pages). The sort below using
long- and short-"i" words is shown as two different sorts (see Figure 5.7).

1. Prepare a collection of 15 to 20 words using the lists on page 119–120 and
    words from reading materials you are using. Be sure to include words that
    have long and short vowel sounds as well as two different spelling patterns
    for the long vowel sound. The sort below has the two sounds for the letter
    "i" (short and long), as well as two patterns for the long-"i" sound (I_E and
    IGH). Have your child make two separate groups: one group for the short
    "i" sound and one for the long "i" sound.

2. Use words, letters, or pictures as headers for the sound sort, and sort as
    usual. If the child is unsure about a word, it can be put in a miscellaneous
    category and revisited later.

3. After all the words have been sorted, ask the child to read down from the
    top and listen for the vowel sound in each word. Ask your child if all the
    words in each column have the same vowel sound.

4. To begin the second step of the sort (the pattern sort), ask your child if he
    sees some words in a column that look like they might "go together" or that
    are "spelled alike." Tell your child to make two columns out of the one to
    create the second sort shown above. Ask your child to tell you how the
    words in each column are now alike. (In the first column, there is only one

FIGURE 5.7. **Two-step word sort with short and long "i."**

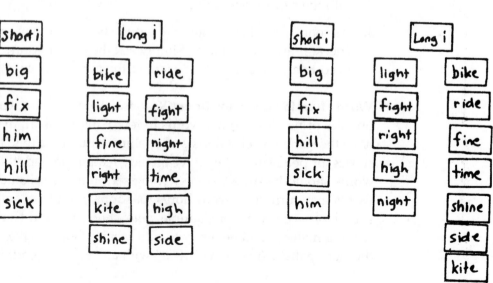

vowel. In the second column, there is a vowel and a silent "e." In the last column, there is a GH in each word.)

5. Ask your child to sort the words again on his own, but start with three columns and sort by sound and pattern at the same time. Discuss and check as usual.

Follow up the two-step pattern sort with a *writing sort* and a *word hunt,* as described on pages 117 and 118.

Observation Guide for the Word Study for Phonics

Ask yourself the following questions to assess how well your student did in the phonics portion of word study. Record your observations on the lesson plan as a guide for future planning.

- How well was your child able to sort the words? (Sorting should be quick and sure after the first time or two.)

- Should you drop back and have fewer categories next time, or can you increase the number of categories? (No more than four at a time is a general rule.)

- Should you repeat the sort, or try new categories at your next session?

- Was your child able to spell the words in the writing sort accurately?

- Were you able to find more words in the word hunt and categorize them?

Evaluating Yourself as a Tutor on the Word Study for Phonics

After several weeks of this level of word study, you might check yourself on the following points. Keep working on these points and you will improve over time!

- Do I set up the category headers and model the first card or two when introducing new categories?

- Do I hand the cards to my child to sort?

- Do I make sure my child can read the words I ask her to sort?

- Do I remain silent during the second sort and allow my child to make mistakes?

- As a conclusion to my sort, do I have my child read down each column to help her find and correct mistakes?

- Do I ask what all the words have in common?

- Does my child sort the words or pictures at least twice?

- Do I include a writing sort?

- During the phonics portion of the lesson, am I well prepared, so we can move quickly through all the activities nearly every lesson?

Early Reader Lesson Plan
Part IV: More Reading or Writing

Revisiting Favorites for More Reading

If there is time at the end of the early reader session, it is pleasant to revisit a favorite book, poem, or an excerpt from a favorite book. The selection does not have to be a long piece but should be one the student chooses and loves to read. Maybe the child enjoys reading it because she loves the expressive language, the message, the topic, or the humor. Perhaps each rereading uncovers something new about the piece, or perhaps it is just like seeing an old friend. In any case, children love to reread their favorite pieces. Revisiting old favorites ends the session on an enjoyable reading note.

More Writing Activities

The writing done for the reading and writing part of the lesson plan is very structured and limited, but there may be occasions that warrant a change of pace. Sometimes, creating personal materials can motivate a child who otherwise may dislike writing. Two forms of more personalized writing are described below.

1. *Writing little books:* Create your own little books that reflect a particular theme (holidays, likes and dislikes, things I can do, and so on) or model a pattern from something you have read. Little books can be easily made by folding two sheets of 8 × 11 paper in half and stapling them in the middle to create an eight-page book. Work together on the composing, writing, and illustrating, maybe adding a page at each tutoring session. Since these books will be reread, you should help with spellings the child can't do on her own. Charla liked the book *Cookie's Week* so much that Phyllis proposed that they write a new version of the story. Charla came up with the story below, writing it over several sessions before taking it home to illustrate and share.

Here is a simple pattern you might adapt for any holiday or season:

Charla's Week

On Monday Charla forgot her lunch money.

On Tuesday Charla fell and scraped her knee.

On Wednesday Charla lost her library book.

On Thursday Charla got sick.

On Friday Charla missed school.

On Saturday Charla felt much better.

Tomorrow is Sunday . . .

Maybe next week will be better.

At Halloween You See	*In Winter I Love to See*
red apples.	snow falling in the night sky.
orange pumpkins.	stockings hanging by the fire.
white ghosts.	bright lights in the window.
green witches.	colorful packages under the tree.
black bats.	smiles on people's faces.

2. *Messages and cards:* Children enjoy writing messages and making cards for each other and for their parents. Creating seasonal cards (Halloween, Valentine's Day) is popular and need not involve a lot of time. Sometimes, children become interested in writing short notes back and forth to other children in the room, and this becomes a wonderful writing activity. You might be able to work out a way that you and the child can write notes to each other. Whenever you come in for a tutoring session to find that your student is absent, write the child a simple, short note in neat block letters that you leave with the teacher, and invite your child to write back.

Best Wishes!

This brings you to the end of the Early Reader Lesson Plan. You may have the pleasure of working with a child starting as an emergent reader and moving into the early stage. If so, you have seen children make progress that should enable them to continue grow in their reading and writing as long as someone, a teacher or another tutor, recognizes where they are and builds on what they know.

Appendix A: Forms for Tutors

Note: We recommend that you enlarge these forms to maximum size when copying them to use.

1. Lesson Plan Forms for the Emergent Reader and the Early Reader (2 pages): Use the appropriate form as described in Chapters 3, 4, and 5 to plan the activities for each tutoring session and record observational notes. Keep these in the tutoring folder as a record of the child's work and progress.

2. Alphabet Cards: These can be copied onto cardstock (preferably) or paper and cut apart to create a set of letters to use for the alphabet activities described in Chapter 4. Alternate forms of A, G, and T are included, because children will often see these in the books they read.

3. Alphabet Chart with Lions: These charts can be used in several ways with emergent readers who need a lot of alphabet work. The child can be asked to name and touch the letters in order, or touch particular letters the tutor might name. The letters can also be colored in as a record of the child's progress in learning the alphabet.

4. Handwriting Chart for Lowercase Letters: This is a good form to keep in the tutors folder, so that when a child needs help on learning the correct formation of a letter, a standard reference is ready. The school where you tutor may have an alternate writing system, and they can supply a copy for you.

5. Small Alphabet Chart and Consonant Sound Chart: A copy of these charts can be attached to the tutoring box or pocket folder for the emergent reader to refer to during reading and writing.

6. Sound Chart for Blends and Digraphs: A copy of this chart can be attached to the tutoring box or kept in the tutor's folder for reference. It will replace the consonant sound chart as the child makes progress.

7. Book List: Keep a copy of this form in the tutor's folder and use it to record the names of the books read by the child and the number of times the book was read.

8. Alphabetized Word-Bank List: Keep a copy of this form in the tutor's folder as a record of the new words that go into the word bank.

9. Word-Bank Records: Use either the rocket ship or the path to the top of the mountain as a visual progress chart of the number of words in the child's word bank. You might count the words every fourth session, draw a line to indicate the number, and let the child color in the space.

10. Common Word Families: List of words to use for the study of word families.

11. "Push It Say It" Letters and Word-Family Cards (3 pages): Make copies of these cards on heavy stock for use in the "Push It Say It" portion of the emergent plan.

12. Template for Word Cards: Words to be used for the sorting of word families and long and short vowel sounds can be written in the spaces on this template and then cut apart for sorting. Coordinators may want to make copies of the sorts they create and keep a file of them for furture use.

13. Timed Repeated Reading Charts: Make copies of these to use as a record of the early reader's accuracy and speed of reading. There are four charts on the form to be used for four different passages. There are three different ways to record the rate, as described in Chapter 5. Indicate what you are counting by circling either "words," "seconds," or "WPM" (words per minute). Indicate the number of reading erors in the space at the bottom.

A.I. Lesson Plan Form for the Emergent Reader

Emergent Plan Student _____ Tutor _____ Date _____ Lesson # _____

Lesson Plan	Description of Planned Activities	Time	Outcomes and Comments
Rereading	Materials:		
Word Study	1. Word Bank: 2. Picture/Word Sort: 3. Writing Sort: 4. Push It Say It:		
Writing	Sentence:		Child's Effort
New Reading	Book: Level: Introduction notes:		Read Book ___ Times

A.1. **Lesson Plan Form for the Early Reader**

Early Plan Student _____ Tutor _____ Date _____ Lesson # _____

Lesson Plan	Description of Planned Activities	Time	Outcomes and Comments
Rereading or Easy Reading	Books: Timed Repeated Reading:		
Reading and Writing	Book: Level: Preview: Written Response Question: Second Response Question:		
Word Study	1. Picture/Word Sort: 3. Writing Sort: 4. Word Hunt:		
Revisit Book or Writing			

A.2. Alphabet Cards

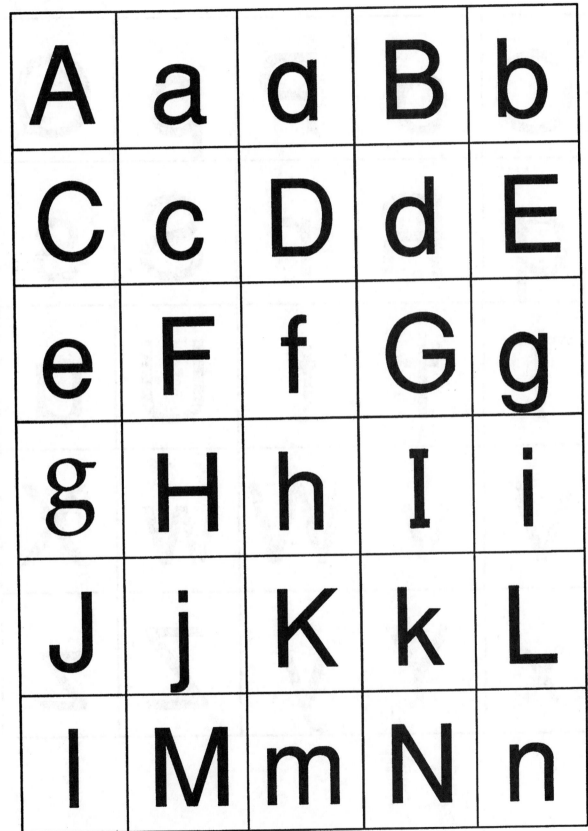

A	a	a	B	b
C	c	D	d	E
e	F	f	G	g
g	H	h	I	i
J	j	K	k	L
l	M	m	N	n

A.2. Alphabet Cards, cont.

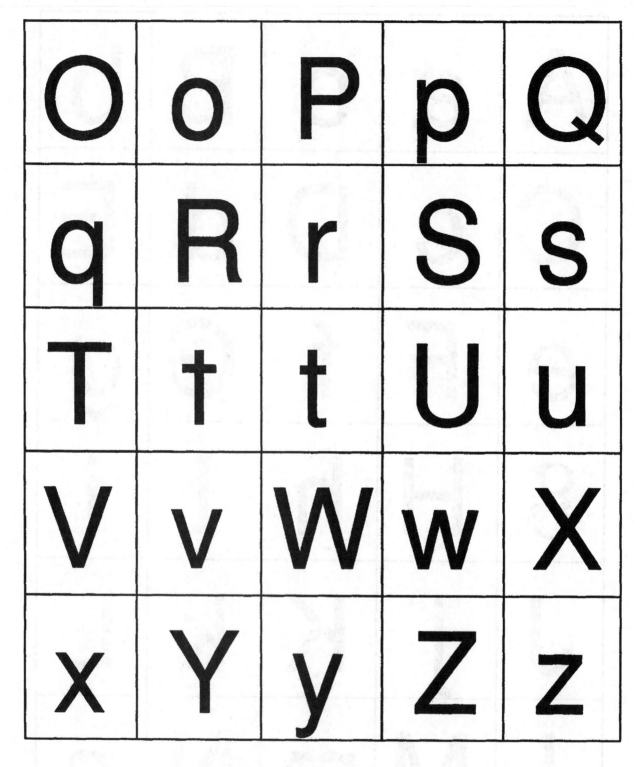

A.3. Alphabet Chart with Lions

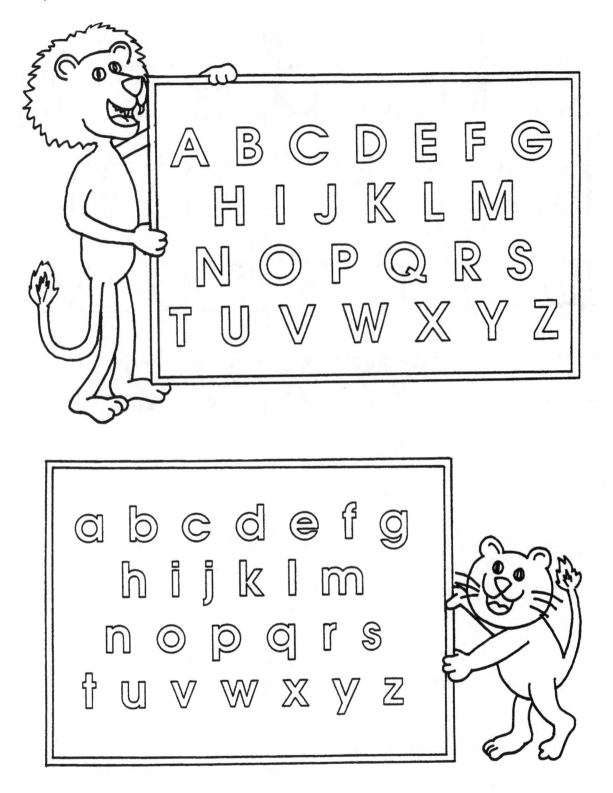

A.4. Handwriting Chart for Lowercase Letters

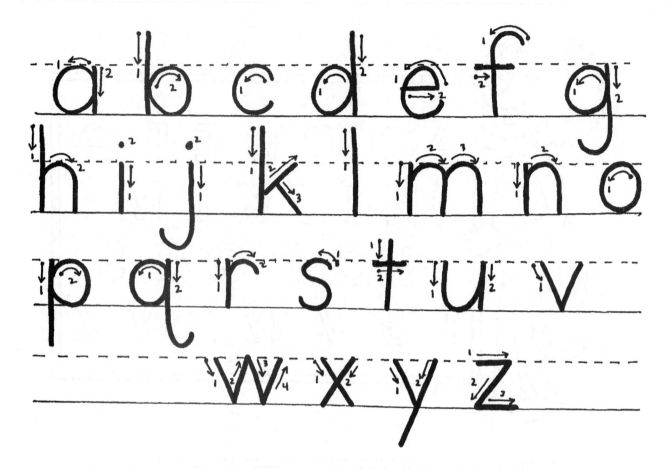

A.5. Small Alphabet Chart and Consonant Sound Chart

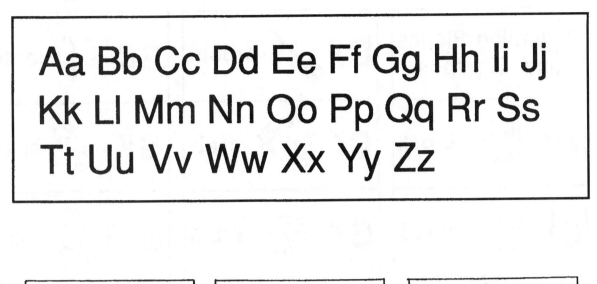

Aa Bb Cc Dd Ee Ff Gg Hh Ii Jj
Kk Ll Mm Nn Oo Pp Qq Rr Ss
Tt Uu Vv Ww Xx Yy Zz

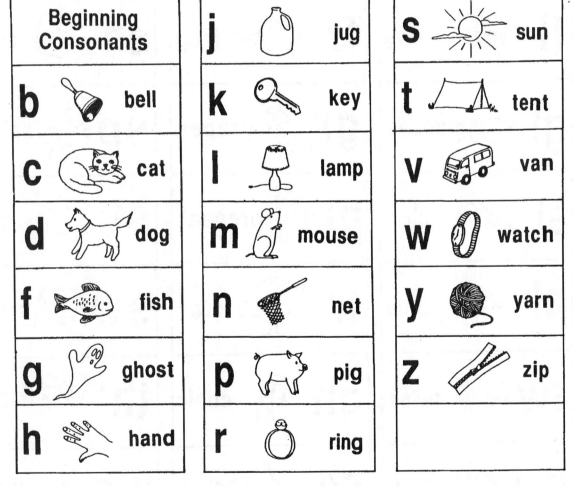

Beginning Consonants					
b	bell	j	jug	s	sun
c	cat	k	key	t	tent
d	dog	l	lamp	v	van
f	fish	m	mouse	w	watch
g	ghost	n	net	y	yarn
h	hand	p	pig	z	zip
		r	ring		

A.6. **Sound Chart for Blends and Digraphs**

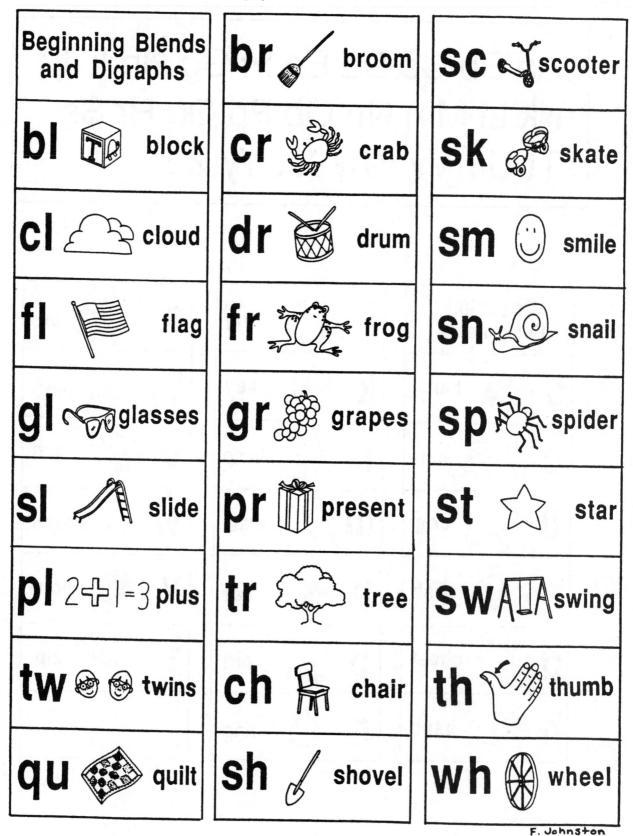

Beginning Blends and Digraphs		
bl block	**br** broom	**sc** scooter
cl cloud	**cr** crab	**sk** skate
fl flag	**dr** drum	**sm** smile
gl glasses	**fr** frog	**sn** snail
sl slide	**gr** grapes	**sp** spider
pl 2+1=3 plus	**pr** present	**st** star
tw twins	**tr** tree	**sw** swing
qu quilt	**ch** chair	**th** thumb
	sh shovel	**wh** wheel

F. Johnston

A.7. Book List

Book List for :_____

1st Date   Name of Book   #Times Read

A.8. Alphabetized Word-Bank List

A	F	M	S
	G		
B		N	T
	H	O	
C			U
	I	P	V
			W
	J		
D	K	Q	
	L	R	X
			Y
E			
			Z

A.9. Word-Bank Records

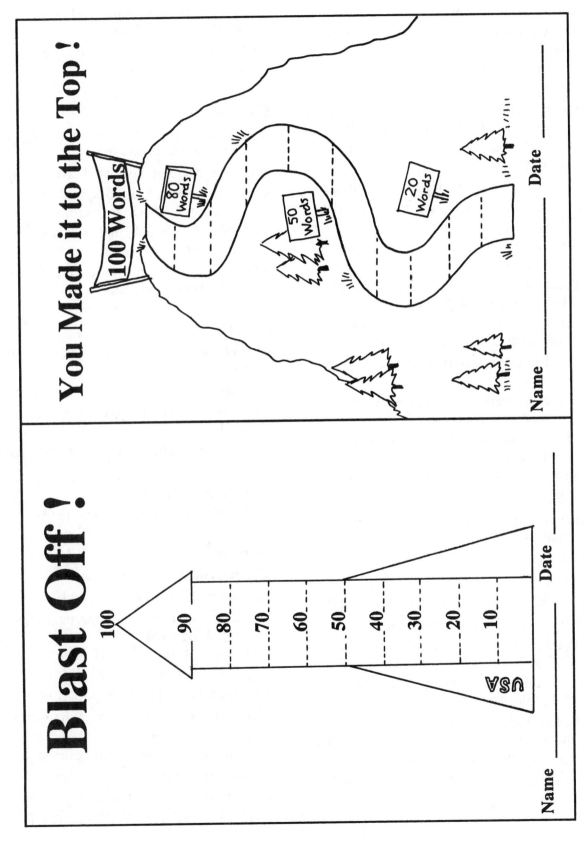

A.10. Common Word Families

Short "a" (and -all and -ar)

-AT: bat, cat, fat, hat, mat, pat, rat, sat, that, flat, brat, chat

-AN: can, fan, man, pan, ran, tan, van, plan, than

-ACK: back, pack, jack, rack, sack, tack, black, quack, crack, track, shack, snack, stack

-AB: cab, dab, jab, nab, lab, tab, blab, crab, scab, stab, grab

-AD: bad, dad, had, mad, pad, sad, rad, glad

-AG: bag, rag, sag, wag, nag, flag, brag, drag, shag, snag

-AM: am, dam, ham, ram, jam, clam, slam, cram, wham, swam

-AP: cap, lap, map, nap, rap, tap, zap, clap, flap, slap, trap, chap, snap

-ASH: bash, cash, dash, hash, mash, rash, sash, flash, trash, crash, smash

-AND: band, hand, land, sand, brand, grand, stand

-ANK: bank, sank, tank, yank, blank, plank, crank, drank, prank, spank, thank

-ALL: ball, call, fall, hall, mall, tall, wall, small, stall

-ANG: bang, fang, hang, sang, rang, clang

-AR: bar, car, far, jar, par, star

-ART: art, cart, dart, mart, part, tart, start, chart, smart

Short "i"

-IT: bit, kit, fit, hit, lit, pit, sit, quit, skit, spit

-IG: big, dig, fig, pig, rig, wig, zig

-ILL: bill, dill, fill, hill, kill, mill, pill, will, drill, grill, chill, skill, spill, still

-IN: bin, fin, pin, tin, win, grin, thin, twin, chin, shin, skin, spin

-ICK: lick, kick, pick, sick, tick, click, slick, quick, trick, chick, flick, brick, stick, thick

-IP: dip, hip, lip, nip, rip, sip, tip, zip, whip, clip, flip, slip, skip, drip, trip, chip, ship,

-INK: ink, link, mink, pink, sink, rink, wink, blink, drink, stink, think

-ING: king, sing, ring, wing, sling, bring, sting, swing, thing

Short "o"

-OT: cot, dot, got, hot, jot, lot, not, pot, rot, blot, slot, plot, shot, spot

-OG: dog, bog, fog, hog, jog, log, clog, frog

-OCK: dock, lock, rock, sock, tock, block, clock, flock, smock, shock

-OB: cob, job, rob, gob, mob, sob, snob, blob, glob, snob

-OP: cop, hop, pop, mop, top, clop, flop, slop, drop, chop, shop, stop

Short "e"

-ET: bet, get, jet, let, met, net, pet, set, wet, vet, fret

-EN: den, hen, men, ten, pen, then, when

-ED: bed, fed, led, red, wed, bled, fled, sled, shed

-ELL: bell, fell, jell, sell, tell, well, shell, smell, spell

-EG: beg, peg, leg, keg

-ECK: deck, neck, peck, wreck, speck, check

Short "u"

-UT: but, cut, gut, hut, nut, rut, shut

-UB: cub, hub, rub, tub, club, grub, snub, stub

-UG: bug, dug, hug, jug, mug, rug, tug, slug, plug, drug, snug

-UCK: buck, duck, luck, suck, tuck, yuck, pluck, cluck, truck, stuck

-UFF: buff, cuff, huff, muff, puff, fluff

-UM: bum, gum, hum, drum, plum, slum, glum, scum, chum

-UN: bun, fun, gun, run, sun, spun, stun

-UP: up, cup, pup

-UMP: bump, jump, dump, hump, lump, pump, rump, plump, stump, thump

A.11. "Push It Say It" Letters and Word-Family Cards

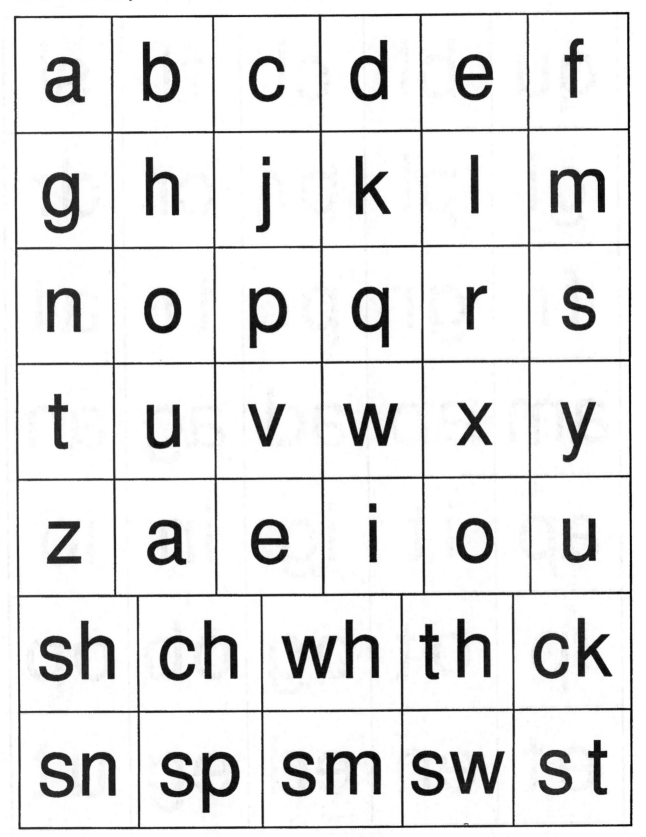

A.11. "Push It Say It" Letters and Word-Family Cards, cont.

qu	bl	cl	fl	sl
gl	pl	br	cr	dr
fr	gr	pr	tr	at
am	ab	ad	ag	an
ap	it	ig	in	id
ip	ot	og	ob	op
et	en	ed	eg	ut

A.11. "Push It Say It" Letters and Word-Family Cards, cont.

ub	ug	um	un	up

ack	ick	ock	uck
eck	ink	ank	unk
ang	ing	ung	ong
all	ill	ell	and
ump	ish	ush	ash
ast	est	ust	uff

A.12. Template for Word Cards

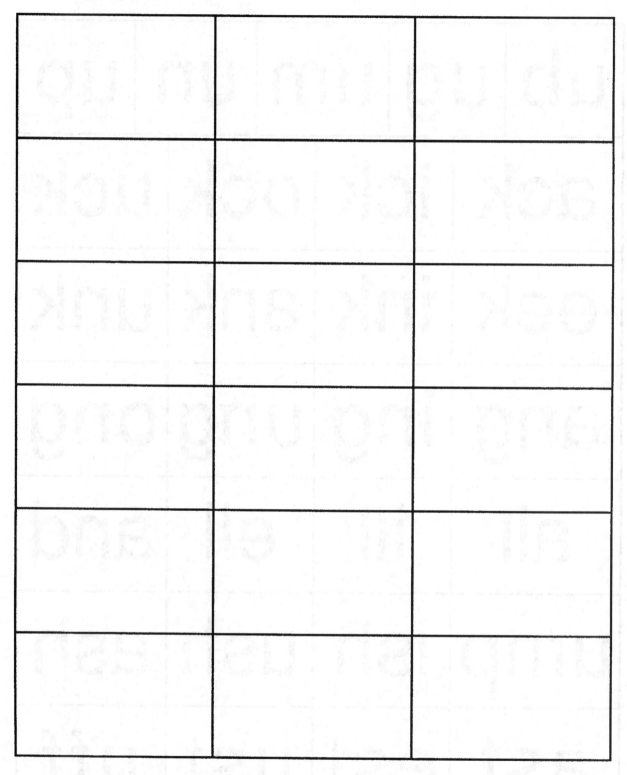

A.13. Timed Repeated Reading Charts

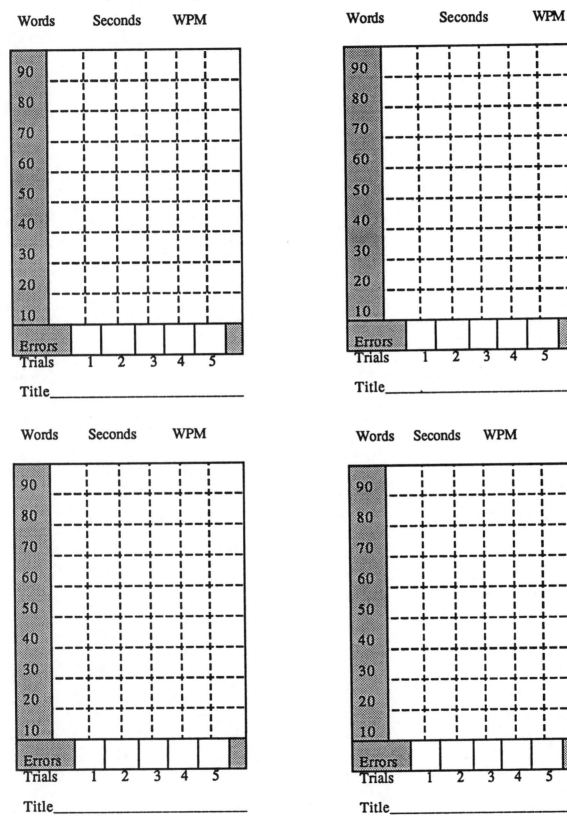

Appendix B: Resources

1. A sample permission letter.

2. Leveled List of Books by Individual Authors: This leveled list has books that are widely available in libraries and bookstores, many by well known authors. The levels have been assigned by Reading Recovery® teachers (10 pages).

3. Leveled List of Books by Phonics Features: This list, prepared by Mary Boylin, has books by phonic elements and by level (when it is known). The publishers are listed in the next section (7 pages).

4. Sources of Series Books: A wide variety of publishers offer little books that are specially designed for emergent and beginning readers. This list is by no means complete, and you may want to consult with local teachers and reading specialists for more ideas. You should also consider what books are being used in the children's classrooms and try to secure materials that are different.

5. Order form for pictures to use in word study for phonics sorts.

6. Information on quantity discounts for *Book Buddies*.

7. Information on training videos for *Book Buddies*.

B.1.   Sample Permission Letter

Any Elementary School
1600 Washington Street
Yourtown, State

September 1, 1997

Dear _____ ,

Your child, _____, has been selected to receive one-on-one tutoring from a volunteer reading tutor two times a week. Each volunteer will work under the direction of Mrs. Miles, the Reading Coordinator, who will work closely with your child's classroom teacher to provide the help your child needs to make good progress in reading. We are very pleased to have this tutorial program at our school.

We may want to videotape your child working with his or her tutor as a way to train other tutors or to interest people in our program. We ask that you give us permission to videotape your child or to take a picture of your child.

Once we have gotten your permission, we will let your know the name of your child's tutor and tell you a little about him or her. We encourage you to come and visit a tutoring session anytime to observe or to meet your child's tutor.

If you have any questions about the tutoring program please call me, Mrs. Miles, or your child's classroom teacher.

Sincerely,

Jennifer Howard, Principal

_____

I give permission for _____ to participate in the volunteer reading tutoring program at Anyschool. I understand that my child may be photographed or videotaped.

_____

Parent or Guardian's Signature

B.2. Leveled List of Trade Books by Individual Authors

Author	Title of Book	RR Level	Publisher
Carle, Eric	*So You Want to Be My Friend*	I	Penguin
Hoban, Tana	*Count and See*	I	Macmillan
Hutchins, Pat	*One Hunter*	I	Greenwillow
MacMillan, Bruce	*Growing Colors*	I	Mondo
Maris, Ron	*My Book*	I	Penguin
Ormerod, Jan	*Sunshine*	I	Lothrop
Wildsmith, Brian	*Applebird*	I	Oxford
Wildsmith, Brian	*Cat on the Mat*	I	Oxford
Carle, Eric	*Have You Seen My Cat?*	2	Putnam
Pienkowsky, Jan	*Colors*	2	Penguin
Tafuri, Nancy	*Have You Seen My Duckling?*	2	Greenwillow
Jonas, Ann	*Now We Can Go*	3	Greenwillow
Moncure, J.	*Hi, Word Bird*	3	Child's World
Steptoe, John	*Baby Says*	3	Morrow
Wildsmith, Brian	*What a Tale*	3	Oxford
Wildsmith, Brian	*Toot, Toot*	3	Oxford
Wildsmith, Brian	*All Fall Down*	3	Oxford
Kalan, Robert	*Rain*	4	Greenwillow
Martin, Bill	*Brown Bear, Brown Bear*	4	Henry Holt & Co.
Mueller, Virginia	*Halloween Mask for Monster*	4	Whitman
Mueller, Virginia	*Playhouse for Monster*	4	Whitman
Peek, Merle	*Roll Over*	4	Clarion
Tafuri, Nancy	*Spots, Feathers, and Curly Tails*	4	Greenwillow
Tuchman, G. & Dieterichs, S.	*Swing, Swing, Swing*	4	Scholastic
Williams, Sue	*I Went Walking*	4	Harcourt Brace
Aruego, Jose	*Look What I Can Do*	5	Silver Burdett Ginn
Brown, R. & Carey, S.	*Hide and Seek*	5	Scholastic
Mueller, Virginia	*Monster and the Baby*	5	Whitman
Peppe, Rodney	*Humpty Dumpty*	5	Penguin (Viking)
Tafuri, Nancy	*Ball Bounced, The*	5	Greenwillow
Wildsmith, Brian	*Animal Shapes*	5	Oxford
Barton, Byron	*Where's Al?*	6	Houghton Mifflin
Carle, Eric	*From Head to Toe*	6	HarperCollins
Carter, David	*How Many Bugs in a Box?*	6	Simon & Schuster
Crews, Donald	*School Bus*	6	Greenwillow
Ginsburg, Mirra	*Chick and the Duckling, The*	6	Macmillan
Jones, Carol	*Old MacDonald Had a Farm*	6	Houghton Mifflin
Lindgren, Barbo	*Sam's Ball*	6	Morrow
Lindgren, Barbo	*Sam's Cookie*	6	Morrow
Lindgren, Barbo	*Sam's Teddy Bear*	6	Morrow
Lindgren, Barbo	*Sam's Wagon*	6	Morrow
Moncure, J.	*Stop! Go! Word Bird*	6	Child's World
Peek, Merle	*Math Is Everywhere*	6	Clarion
Poulet, Virginia	*Blue Bug's Vegetable Garden*	6	Children's Press
Poulet, Virginia	*Blue Bug and the Bullies*	6	Children's Press
Poulet, Virginia	*Blue Bug Goes to School*	6	Children's Press

B.2.   **Leveled List of Trade Books by Individual Authors, cont.**

Author	Title of Book	RR Level	Publisher
Rounds, Glen	Old MacDonald Had a Farm	6	Holiday House
Salem, L. & Stewart, J.	Cat Who Loved Red, The	6	Seedling Publications
Salem, L. & Stewart, J.	It's Game Day	6	Seedling Publications
Wylie, J. & D.	Funny Old Man & Funny Old Woman	6	Children's Press
Wylie, J. & D.	Fishy Color Story	6	Scott Foresman
Adams, Pam	There Were Ten in the Bed	7	Child's Play
Crews, Donald	Flying	7	Greenwillow
Kraus, Robert	Happy Egg	7	Scholastic
Moncure, J.	No, No, Word Bird	7	Child's World
Poulet, Virginia	Blue Bug's Book Of Colours	7	Children's Press
Salem, L. & Stewart, J.	What's for Dinner?	7	Seedling Publications
Shaw, Charles	It Looked Like Spilt Milk	7	HarperCollins
Berenstain, Stan & Jan	Inside, Outside, Upside Down	8	Random House
Christelow, Eileen	Five Little Monkeys Jumping On...	8	Penguin
Cummings, Pat	Show And Tell	8	Scholastic
Eastmon, P. D.	Go, Dog, Go!	8	Random House
Hill, Eric	Where's Spot?	8	Putnam
Jonas, Ann	Where Can It Be?	8	Greenwillow
Kraus, Robert	Herman the Helper	8	Simon & Schuster
Langstaff, John	Oh a Hunting We Will Go	8	Macmillan
Mayer, Mercer	All By Myself	8	Donovan
Perkins, Al	Ear Book	8	Random House
Perkins, Al	Nose Book	8	Random House
Wylie, J. & D.	More or Less Fish Story	8	Children's Press
Adams, Pam	This Old Man	9	Child's Play
Asch, Frank	Just Like Daddy	9	Simon & Schuster
Campbell, Rod	Dear Zoo	9	Macmillan
Campbell, Rod	Oh Dear!	9	Macmillan (Four Winds)
Galdone, Paul	Cat Goes Fiddle-i-fee	9	Clarion
Henkes, Kevin	Shhh	9	Greenwillow
Hutchins, Pat	Rosie's Walk	9	Macmillan
Lilgard, D. & Zimmerman, J.	Frog's Lunch	9	Scholastic
Maris, Ron	Are You There, Bear?	9	Greenwillow
Medearis, A., & Keeter, S.	Harry's House	9	Scholastic
Moncure, J.	Hide and Seek, Word Bird	9	Child's World
Moncure, J.	Watch Out, Word Bird	9	Child's World
Raffi	Wheels on the Bus	9	Random House
Reese, Bob	Huzzard Buzzard	9	Children's Press
West, Colin	Pardon?	9	HarperCollins
Westcott, Nadine	Lady with the Alligator Purse, The	9	Little, Brown
Ziefert, Harriet	Wheels on the Bus	9	Random House
Ziefert, Harriet	Here Comes the Bus	9	Penguin
Brown, Ruth	Dark, Dark Tale	10	Penguin
Charles, Donald	Calico Cat at the Zoo	10	Children's Press
DeRegniers, B.S.	Going for a Walk	10	HarperCollins
Gernstein, Nordicai	Roll Over!	10	Random House (Crown)

Author	Title of Book	RR Level	Publisher
Ginsburg, Mirra	*Across the Stream*	10	Greenwillow
Hall, N. & Robinson, A.	*My Holiday Diary*	10	Around the World
Hurd, Edith Thatcher	*Johnny Lion's Rubber Boots*	10	HarperCollins
Krauss, Ruth	*Is This You?*	10	Scholastic
Moncure, J.	*Word Bird Builds a City*	10	Child's World
Moncure, J.	*Word Bird Shapes*	10	Child's World
Poulet, Virginia	*Blue Bug Goes to the Library*	10	Children's Press
Rockwell, Anne	*Cars*	10	Penguin
Rockwell, Harlow	*My Kitchen*	10	Greenwillow
Salem, L. & Stewart, J.	*Notes from Mom*	10	Seedling Publications
Seuss, Dr.	*Foot Book*	10	Random House
Stadler, John	*Hooray for Snail*	10	HarperCollins
Ward, Cindy	*Cookie's Week*	10	Putnam
Wylie, J. & D.	*Fishy Alphabet Story*	10	Children's Press
Ziefert, Harriet	*Harry Takes a Bath*	10	Penguin
Ziefert, Harriet	*Thank You, Nicky!*	10	Penguin
Ahlberg, A. & J.	*Each Peach Pear Plum*	11	Penguin
Barton, Byron	*Dinosaurs, Dinosaurs*	11	HarperCollins
Dorros, Arthur	*Alligator Shoes*	11	Penguin
Gelman, Rita	*More Spaghetti, I Say!*	11	Scholastic
Hill, Eric	*Spot's First Walk*	11	Putnam
Jonas, Ann	*When You Were a Baby*	11	Greenwillow
Mack, Stan	*Ten Bears in My Bed*	11	Random House
Mayer, Mercer	*Just for You*	11	Donovan
Mayer, Mercer	*Just Me and My Baby Sister*	11	Donovan
Minarik, E. H.	*Cat and Dog*	11	HarperCollins
Reese, Bob	*Critter Race*	11	Children's Press
Reese, Bob	*Scary Larry*	11	Children's Press
Reese, Bob	*Tweedledee, Tumbleweed*	11	Children's Press
Rockwell, Anne	*Boats*	11	Penguin (Dutton)
Shaw, Nancy	*Sheep in a Jeep*	11	Houghton Mifflin
Bonsall, Crosby	*Day I Had to Play with My Sister, The*	12	HarperCollins
Bonsall, Crosby	*Mine's the Best*	12	HarperCollins
Brandenberg, F.	*I Wish I Was Sick, Too!*	12	Mulberry Books
Bunting, E. & Sloan-Childers, E.	*Rabbit's Party*	12	Scholastic
Crews, Donald	*Ten Black Dots*	12	Greenwillow
Gelman, Rita	*Why Can't I Fly?*	12	Scholastic
Hutchins, Pat	*Titch*	12	Macmillan
Keller, Holly	*Ten Sleepy Sheep*	12	Greenwillow
Kline, Suzy	*Shine Sun*	12	Whitman
Kraus, Robert	*Boris Bad Enough*	12	Simon & Schuster
Krauss, Ruth	*Carrot Seed*	12	HarperCollins
Long, Erlene	*Gone Fishing*	12	Houghton Mifflin
Shulevitz, Uri	*One Monday Morning*	12	Macmillan
Stadler, John	*Three Cheers for Hippo*	12	HarperCollins (Crowell)
Taylor, Judy	*My Dog*	12	Macmillan
Van, Laan, Nancy	*Big Fat Worm, The*	12	Random House

B.2. **Leveled List of Trade Books by Individual Authors, cont.**

Author	Title of Book	RR Level	Publisher
Wescott, Nadine	*Peanut Butter and Jelly*	12	Penguin
Ziefert, Harriet	*Jason's Bus Ride*	12	Penguin
Ziefert, Harriet	*Mike and Tony: Best Friends*	12	Penguin
Ziefert, Harriet	*New House for Mole and Mouse*	12	Penguin
Ziefert, Harriet	*Nicky Upstairs and Downstairs*	12	Penguin
Barton, Byron	*Buzz, Buzz, Buzz*	13	Macmillan
Berenstain, Stan & Jan	*Old Hat, New Hat*	13	Random House
Bucknall, Caroline	*One Bear All Alone*	13	Penguin
Jonas, Ann	*Two Bear Cubs*	13	Greenwillow
Joyce, William	*George Shrinks*	13	HarperCollins
Kraus, Robert	*Whose Mouse Are You?*	13	Macmillan
Reese, Bob	*Rapid Robert, Road Runner*	13	Children's Press
Rockwell, Anne	*Tool Box*	13	Macmillan
Sendak, Maurice	*Seven Little Monsters*	13	HarperCollins
Ziefert, Harriet	*No Ball Games Here*	13	Penguin
Adams, Pam	*There Was an Old Lady Who*	14	Child's Play
Aliki	*We Are Best Friends*	14	Mulberry Books
Barchas, Sarah	*I Was Walking Down the Road*	14	Scholastic
Barton, Byron	*Building a House*	14	Greenwillow
Brown, Margaret Wise	*Goodnight Moon*	14	HarperCollins
Butler, Dorothy	*My Brown Bear Barney*	14	Greenwillow
Gelman, Rita	*Cats and Mice*	14	Scholastic
Hutchins, Pat	*You'll Soon Grow into Them, Titch*	14	Greenwillow
Hutchins, Pat	*What Game Shall We Play?*	14	Sundance
Johnson, Crockett	*Picture for Harold's Room*	14	HarperCollins
Kraus, Robert	*Come Out and Play, Little Mouse*	14	Greenwillow
Kraus, Robert	*Where Are You Going, Little Mouse?*	14	Greenwillow
Kraus, Robert	*Owliver*	14	Simon & Schuster
Seuling, Barbara	*Teeny, Tiny Woman*	14	Random House
Taylor, Judy	*My Cat*	14	Macmillan
Wildsmith, Brian	*Animal Tricks*	14	Oxford
Ziefert, Harriet	*Clean House for Mole and Mouse*	14	Scholastic
Barton, Bryon	*Airport*	15	HarperCollins
Brown, Marc	*Spooky Riddles*	15	Random House
Cebulash, M. & Ford, G.	*Willie's Wonderful Pet*	15	Scholastic
Eastman, P.D.	*Are You My Mother?*	15	Random House
Eastman, P.D.	*Big Dog, Little Dog*	15	Random House
Fox, Mem	*Hattie and the Fox*	15	Macmillan
Friskey, Margaret	*Indian Two Feet and His Horse*	15	Children's Press
Gibson, A. & Meyer, K.	*Nana's Place*	15	Scholastic
Hayes, Sara & Craig, H.	*This Is the Bear*	15	Penguin
Hurd, Edith Thatcher	*Come and Have Fun*	15	HarperCollins
Jonas, Ann	*Reflections*	15	Greenwillow
Mayer, Mercer	*Just a Mess*	15	Donovan
Mayer, Mercer	*Just Grandma and Me*	15	Donovan
McPhail, David	*Fix-it*	15	Penguin (Dutton)

Author	Title of Book	RR Level	Publisher
Nodset, Joan	*Who Took the Farmer's Hat?*	15	Scholastic
Rosen, Michael	*We're Going on a Bear Hunt*	15	Macmillan
Sendak, Maurice	*Alligators All Around*	15	HarperCollins
Serfozo, Mary	*Who Wants One?*	15	Macmillan
Seuss, Dr.	*I Can Read with My Eyes Shut*	15	Random House
Seuss, Dr.	*Great Day for Up*	15	Random House
Seuss, Dr.	*Hop on Pop*	15	Random House
Wood, Don & Audrey	*Napping House, The*	15	Harcourt
Wood, Don & Audrey	*The Little Mouse, The Red Ripe Strawberry and the Big Hungry Bear*	15	Child's Play
Allen, Pamela	*Bertie the Bear*	16	Putnam
Bennett, Jill	*Teeny Tiny*	16	Putnam
Berenstain, Stan & Jan	*Bike Lesson*	16	Random House
Brown, Marcia	*Three Billy Goats Gruff*	16	Harcourt
Carle, Eric	*Very Busy Spider, The*	16	Putnam
Cook, Bamadine	*Little Fish That Got Away*	16	Scholastic
Freeman, Don	*Rainbow of My Own*	16	Penguin
Galdone, Paul	*Little Yellow Chicken*	16	Clarion
Galdone, Paul	*Henny Penny*	16	Scholastic
Heilbroner, Joan	*Robert the Rose Horse*	16	Random House
Hill, Eric	*Spot's Birthday*	16	Putnam
Hoff, Syd	*Albert the Albatross*	16	HarperCollins
Hutchins, Pat	*Happy Birthday Sam*	16	Greenwillow
Hutchins, Pat	*Tidy Titch*	16	Greenwillow
Hutchins, Pat	*Goodnight Owl*	16	Macmillan
Jonas, Ann	*Quilt, The*	16	Greenwillow
Jonas, Ann	*Triceratops on the Farm*	16	Greenwillow
Kent, Jack	*Fat and Thin*	16	Scholastic
Kovalski, Mary Ann	*Wheels on the Bus*	16	Little, Brown
Kraus, Robert	*Leo the Late Bloomer*	16	Simon & Schuster
Kuskin, Karla	*Just Like Everyone Else*	16	HarperCollins
Mayer, Mercer	*Just Me and My Dad*	16	Donovan
Mayer, Mercer	*Just Me and My Puppy*	16	Donovan
Mayer, Mercer	*There's a Nightmare in My Closet*	16	Penguin
McLeod, Emilie	*Bears' Bicycle*	16	Little, Brown
Minarik, E. & H.	*Kiss for Little Bear*	16	HarperCollins
Ormerod, Jan	*Story of Chicken Licken*	16	Lothrop
Rice, Eve	*Benny Bakes a Cake*	16	Greenwillow
Rockwell, Anne	*Trucks*	16	Penguin
Sadler, Marilyn	*It's Not Easy Being a Bunny*	16	Random House
Wells, Rosemary	*Noisy Nora*	16	Scholastic
Wood, Don & Audrey	*Big Kick, The*	16	Scholastic
Ahlberg, A. & J.	*Funny Bones*	17	Greenwillow
Asch, Frank	*Last Puppy, The*	17	Simon & Schuster
Berenstain, Stan & Jan	*He Bear, She Bear*	17	Random House
Bonsall, Crosby	*And I Mean It, Stanley*	17	HarperCollins
Bornstein, Ruth	*Little Gorilla*	17	Clarion
Brown, Margaret Wise	*Little Fireman*	17	HarperCollins

B.2.   Leveled List of Trade Books by Individual Authors, cont.

Author	Title of Book	RR Level	Publisher
Flack, Marjorie	Ask Mr. Bear	17	MacMillan
Galdone, Paul	Three Billy Goats Gruff	17	Clarion
Hill, Eric	Spot's First Christmas	17	Putnam
Hoff, Syd	Horse in Harry's Room	17	HarperCollins
Hurd, Edith Thatcher	Johnny Lion's Book	17	HarperCollins
Hutchins, Pat	Doorbell Rang, The	17	Greenwillow
Hutchins, Pat	Clocks and More Clocks	17	Macmillan
Isadora, Rachel	Max	17	Macmillan
Johnson, Crockett	Harold and Purple Crayon	17	HarperCollins
Kraus, Robert	Milton the Early Riser	17	Simon & Schuster
LeSeig, Theo	Ten Apples up on Top	17	Random House
Lobel, Arnold	Mouse Soup	17	HarperCollins
Lobel, Arnold	Mouse Tales	17	HarperCollins
Mayer, Mercer	There's an Alligator under My Bed	17	Penguin
Mayer, Mercer	There's Something in My Attic	17	Penguin
McGovern, Ann	Stone Soup	17	Scholastic
Parkinson, Kathy	Farmer in the Dell	17	Whitman
Perkins, Al	Hand, Hand, Fingers, Thumb	17	Random House
Roy, Ron	Three Ducks Went Wandering	17	Clarion
Thaler, Mike	There's a Hippopotamus Under …	17	Avon
Udry, Janice May	Let's Be Enemies	17	HarperCollins
Alexander, Martha	Blackboard Bear	18	Penguin
Asch, Frank	Bear Shadow	18	Simon & Schuster
Bridwell, Norman	Clifford the Big Red Dog	18	Scholastic
Bridwell, Norman	Clifford and the Small Red Puppy	18	Scholastic
Carle, Eric	Very Hungry Caterpillar, The	18	Putnam
Cummings, Pat	Jimmy Lee Did It	18	Lothrop
Dabcovich, Lydia	Mrs. Huggins and Her Hen, Hanna	18	Penguin (Dutton)
Degen, Bruce	Jamberry	18	HarperCollins
DePaola, Tomie	Charlie Needs a Cloak	18	Simon & Schuster
Eastman, P.D.	Sam and the Firefly	18	Random House
Eastmon, P.D.	Best Nest	18	Random House
Emberly, Barbara & Ed	Drummer Hoff	18	Simon & Schuster
Farley, Walter	Little Black, a Pony	18	Random House
Gibson, A. & Akiyam, M.	Little One Inch	18	Scholastic
Hoff, Syd	Little Chief	18	HarperCollins
Holl, Adelaide	Rain Puddle	18	Lothrop
Keats, E.J.	Snowy Day, The	18	Scholastic
Lear, Edward	Owl and the Pussycat	18	Scholastic
Lionni, Leo	Little Blue and Little Yellow	18	Astor–Honor
Littledale, Freya	Boy Who Cried Wolf, The	18	Scholastic
Lobel, Arnold	Owl at Home	18	HarperCollins
Marshall, E. & Marshall J.	Fox and His Friends	18	Scholastic
Mayer, Mercer	When I Get Bigger	18	Donovan
Mayer, Mercer	I Was So Mad	18	Donovan (Golden Press)
Mayer, Mercer	Me, Too!	18	Donovan (Golden Press)

Author	Title of Book	RR Level	Publisher
Minarik, E. H.	*Little Bear*	18	HarperCollins
Nims, Bonnie	*Where Is the Bear?*	18	Whitman
Numeroff, L. J.	*If You Give a Mouse a Cookie*	18	Scholastic
Preller, J. & Scherer, J.	*Wake Me in Spring*	18	Scholastic
Rice, Eve	*Sam Who Never Forgets*	18	Greenwillow
Seuss, Dr.	*Cat in the Hat*	18	Random House
Van Leeuwen, Jan	*More Tales of Amanda Pig*	18	Penguin (Dial)
Van Leeuwen, Jan	*More Tales of Oliver Pig*	18	Penguin (Dial)
Wallner, John	*City Mouse—Country Mouse*	18	Scholastic
Bogart J. & Wilson, J.	*Daniel's Dog*	19	Scholastic
Bonsall, Crosby	*Piggle*	19	HarperCollins
Brown, Ruth	*Big Sneeze, The*	19	Lothrop
Bumingham, John	*Mr. Gumpy's Motor Car*	19	HarperCollins (Crowell)
Bumingham, John	*Mr. Gumpy's Outing*	19	Henry Holt & Co.
Byars, Betsy	*Go and Hush the Baby*	19	HarperCollins
Elkin, Benjamin	*Six Foolish Fisherman*	19	Children's Press
Gumey, Nancy	*King, the Mice and the Cheese*	19	Random House
Hutchins, Pat	*Surprise Party*	19	Macmillan
Lobel, Arnold	*Frog and Toad Are Friends*	19	HarperCollins
Lobel, Arnold	*Frog and Toad Together*	19	HarperCollins
Minarik, E. H.	*Father Bear Comes Home*	19	HarperCollins
Murphy, Jill	*What Next, Baby Bear*	19	Penguin
Oppenheim, Joanne	*You Can't Catch Me*	19	Houghton Mifflin
Stevens, Janet	*Three Billy Goats Gruff*	19	Harcourt
Allard, Harry	*Miss Nelson is Missing*	20	Houghton Mifflin
Allen, Pamela	*Who Sank the Boat?*	20	Putnam (Coward)
Asch, Frank	*Happy Birthday, Moon*	20	Simon & Schuster
Berenstain, Stan & Jan	*Bears and the Missing*	20	Random House
Crowe, Robert	*Tyler Toad and the Thunder*	20	Penguin
DePaola, Tomie	*Art Lesson, The*	20	Putnam
Galdone, Paul	*Three Little Pigs*	20	Clarion
Galdone, Paul	*Gingerbread Boy, The*	20	Clarion
Galdone, Paul	*Over in the Meadow*	20	Simon & Schuster
Hall, N. & Robinson, A.	*What a Funny Thing to Do*	20	Around the World
Hurd, Edith Thatcher	*Stop, Stop*	20	HarperCollins
Hutchins, Pat	*Don't Forget the Bacon*	20	Greenwillow
Hutchins, Pat	*One-Eyed Jake*	20	Greenwillow
Hutchins, Pat	*Wind Blew, The*	20	Macmillan
Keats, Ezra Jack	*Whistle for Willie*	20	Penguin (Puffin)
Lewis, T.P.	*Hill of Fire*	20	HarperCollins
Littledale, Freya	*Magic Fish*	20	Scholastic
Lobel, Arnold	*Uncle Elephant*	20	HarperCollins
Lobodkina, Esphyr	*Caps for Sale*	20	HarperCollins
Sendak, Maurice	*Chicken Soup with Rice*	20	HarperCollins
Zolotow, Charlotte	*I Know a Lady*	20	Greenwillow

B.3. **Leveled List of Books by Phonics Features—Books by Beginning Consonants**

Title of Book	Publisher	RR Level	Phonics Feature
My Monster and Me	Ready Readers—MCP	2	m
The Chocolate Cake	Story Box—Wright Group	2	m
Faces	Sunshine—Wright Group	1	m
My Family	Sunshine—Wright Group	1	m
Monster Mop	Ready Readers—MCP	1–3	m
We Are Singing	Ready Readers—MCP	2	s
Space Journey	Sunshine—Wright Group	1	s
The Storm	Sunshine—Wright Group	1	s
A Picnic in the Sand	Ready Readers—MCP	1–3	s
School Lunch	Ready Readers—MCP	1–3	s, m
Time For Lunch	Ready Readers—MCP	1–3	f
As Fast as a Fox	Ready Readers—MCP	5	f
Two Turtles	Ready Readers—MCP	1–3	t
Terrific Shoes	Ready Readers—MCP	3	t
If You Meet a Dragon	Story Box—Wright Group	3	t
Teeny, Tiny Tina	Literacy 2000—Rigby	3	t
Who Is Ready	Ready Readers—MCP	3	r
Rain	Easy Phonics Readers—CTP	3	r
Red Or Blue?	Ready Readers—MCP	1–3	r
Story Time	Ready Readers—MCP	1–3	d
Who Made That	Ready Readers—MCP	3	d
Look Closer	Ready Readers—MCP	1–3	l
Where Do They Live?	Ready Readers—MCP	3	l
Let's Move	Ready Readers—MCP	2	l, d
Good Girl	Ready Readers—MCP	1–3	g
Goose Chase	Ready Readers—MCP	5	g
Where Do We Go?	Ready Readers—MCP	1–3	g, t
Up They Go	Ready Readers—MCP	1–3	h, d
How to Make a Hen House	Ready Readers—MCP	1–3	h
Too Much Ketchup	Ready Readers—MCP	5	h
Where Can a Hippo Hide?	Ready Readers—MCP	5	h
Can You Find It?	Ready Readers—MCP	1–3	c, f
The Cat Came Back	Ready Readers—MCP	1–3	c
I Like to Count	Ready Readers—MCP	3	c
One Bee Got on the Bus	Ready Readers—MCP	3	b
All Fall Down	Oxford	3	b
Buttons Buttons	Easy Phonics Readers—CTP	2	b
Every Morning	Twig—Wright Group	3	b
Buffy	Literacy 2000—Rigby	2	b
The Bath	Ready Readers—MCP	1–3	b
My Room	Ready Readers—MCP	1–3	b, r
Socks	Ready Readers—MCP	1–3	n
Nanny Goat's Nap	Ready Readers—MCP	4	n, g
Keep Out!	Ready Readers—MCP	1–3	k
Kangaroo in the Kitchen	Ready Readers—MCP	5	k, w
All Wet!	Ready Readers—MCP	1–3	w

Title of Book	Publisher	RR Level	Phonics Feature
Wilma's Wagon	Ready Readers—MCP	5	w
Jan Can Juggle	Ready Readers—MCP	1–3	j
Pat's Perfect Pizza	Ready Readers—MCP	3	p
Pink Pig	Ready Readers—MCP	1–3	p
Where Is It?	Ready Readers—MCP	1–3	p, n, b
Zebra's Yellow Van	Ready Readers—MCP	1–3	y, z
Queen on a Quilt	Ready Readers—MCP	1–3	qu
Vultures on Vacation	Ready Readers—MCP	4	f, w, k, j, h, v
The Party	Ready Readers—MCP	5	m, s, t, r, b
Yes, I Can	Ready Readers—MCP	5	b, d, g, m, s

B.3. **Leveled List of Books by Phonics Features—Books by Word Families**

Title of Book	Publisher	RR Level	Phonics Feature
What Is under the Hat?	Ready Readers—MCP	1–3	-at
Cat on the Mat	Oxford	1	-at
That Fly	Ready Readers—MCP	2	-at
Mat	Bob Books—Scholastic		-at
Sam	Bob Books—Scholastic		-at
The Hat	Ready Readers—MCP	1–3	-at
My Cap	Teacher Created Materials		-ap, -at
Eggs	Ready Readers—MCP	1–3	-an
Dan, the Flying Man	Story Box—Wright Group	4	-an
Mac	Bob Books—Scholastic		-ag
Bags, Cans, Pots and Pans	Ready Readers—MCP	4	-an, ag
What Will You Pack?	Ready Readers—MCP	1–3	-ap
Haddie's Caps	Ready Readers—MCP	6	-ad, ap
My Twin!	Ready Readers—MCP	1–3	-in
Will Bill?	Teacher Created Materials		-ill, -ip
Mr. Fin's Trip	Ready Readers—MCP	7	-ip, -in, -it
Mama Hen, Come Quick	Ready Readers—MCP	1–3	-ick
Stop That	Ready Readers—MCP	3	-at, -ig
Jig and Mag	Bob Books—Scholastic		-ag, -ig
Jog, Frog, Jog	School Zone	7	-og
Lost in the Fog	Ready Readers—MCP	5	-og
Fox on the Box	School Zone	4	-ox
Stop!	Ready Readers—MCP	1–3	-op
Can a Cow Hop?	Ready Readers—MCP	5	-op. -ot
Dot and the Dog	Bob Books—Scholastic		-ag, -ot*
Dot and Mit	Bob Books—Scholastic		-at, -it, -ot
The Toy Box	Ready Readers—MCP	1–3	-ock
Dot's Pot	Teacher Created Materials		-ot, -ox, -og, -op, -ock
My Clock Is Sick	Ready Readers—MCP	5	-ack, -ick, -ock
Gum on the Drum	School Zone	8	-um
Little House	Ready Readers—MCP	1–3	-ug
Good Night, Little Bug	Ready Readers—MCP	6	-un, -ug
A Nut Pie for Jud	Ready Readers—MCP	6	-ut, -ud
Eight Friends in All	Ready Readers—MCP	6	-at, -ot, -um, -all
The Merry-Go-Round	Ready Readers—MCP	4	-an, -in, -on, -un
Sheep's Bell	Ready Readers—MCP	1–3	-ell
Ted's Red Sled	Ready Readers—MCP	6	-ed
Going Fishing	Ready Readers—MCP	1–3	-et
Brett, My Pet	Teacher Created Materials		-et
The Family Tree	Ready Readers—MCP	12	-ed, -et
Ben's Pets	Ready Readers—MCP	3	-et, -en
Nine Men Chase a Hen	School Zone		-et, -en
Peg and Ted	Bob Books—Scholastic		-ed, -et, -en

Title of Book	Publisher	RR Level	Phonics Feature
A Big, Big Box	Ready Readers—MCP	1–3	-en, -ox, -ick, -at
When We Are Big	Ready Readers—MCP	7	-at, -an, -ad, -et, -en
Cat Traps	Step into Reading		-at, -ap, -ack, -ig, -ish, -og, -ug, -uck, -et
Hop on Pop	Dr. Seuss	15	-op, -ed, -at, -ad, -all, -ill

B.3.   **Leveled List of Books by Phonics Features—Books by Blends and Digraphs**

Title of Book	Publisher	RR Level	Phonics Feature
Sally's Spaceship	Ready Readers—MCP	7	s blends
Scat Cat	Ready Readers—MCP		s blends
Miss Swiss	Ready Readers—MCP		s blends
My Lost Top	Ready Readers—MCP	7	initial and final s blends
Blast Off!	Ready Readers—MCP	9	l blends
Glenda the Lion	Ready Readers—MCP	7	l blends
Planting a Garden	Ready Readers—MCP	7	l blends
Glen Wit	Ready Readers—MCP		l blends
Glub Glub	Ready Readers—MCP		l blends
A Fun Place to Eat	Ready Readers—MCP	7	l, s blends
Roll Out the Red Rug	Ready Readers—MCP	7	r blends
At the Track	Ready Readers—MCP	8	r blends
Brag Brag Brag	Ready Readers—MCP		r blends
Here Comes the Bride	Ready Readers—MCP		r blends
The River Grows	Ready Readers—MCP	8	r, l, s blends
At Night	Literacy 2000—Rigby	5	r, l, s blends
I Can Jump	Sunshine—Wright Group	3	r, l, s blends
Where Are They Going?	Story Box—Wright Group	3	r, l, s blends
Poor Old Polly	Story Box—Wright Group	10	r, l, s blends
At the Pond	Ready Readers—MCP		initial and final r, l, s blends
Hunk of Junk	Ready Readers—MCP		initial and final r, l, s blends, nasals
That Pig Can't Do a Thing	Ready Readers—MCP	10	nasals
She Said	Ready Readers—MCP	1–3	sh digraph
Shell Shopping	Ready Readers—MCP	9	sh digraph
Silvia's Soccer Game	Ready Readers—MCP	9	sh digraph
What Is This?	Ready Readers—MCP	1–3	th digraph
Five Little Dinosaurs	Ready Readers—MCP	8	th digraph
Chocolate-chip Cookies	Ready Readers—MCP	1–3	ch digraph
Cat Chat	Ready Readers—MCP	9	ch digraph
Whale Watch	Ready Readers—MCP	1–3	wh digraph
Humpback Whales	Ready Readers—MCP	9	wh digraph
Three White Sheep	Ready Readers—MCP	1–3	initial sh, th, ch, wh
Something to Munch	Ready Readers—MCP	8	final ch, th, sh digraphs
Noises	Literacy 2000—Rigby	8	initial and final ch, th, sh digraphs
Rush, Rush, Rush	Ready Readers—MCP	8	initial and final ch, th, sh digraphs
Where Is Nancy?	Literacy 2000—Rigby	7	initial and final wh, th, sh digraphs
Stan Packs	Ready Readers—MCP	8	initial blends and digraphs
Dragon's Lunch	Ready Readers—MCP	9	nasals
Walking, Walking	Twig—Wright Group	4	initial and final blends and digraphs
In the Tall, Tall Grass	Henry Holt		initial and final blends and digraphs
Lunch	Henry Holt		initial and final blends and digraphs
In the Small, Small Pond	Henry Holt		initial and final blends and digraphs

B.3. Leveled List of Books by Phonics Features—Books by Short Vowels

Title of Book	Publisher	RR Level	Phonics Feature
The Ant	Ready Readers—MCP	7	short a
Sam and Al	Phonics Practice Reader—MCP		short a
Max	Phonics Practice Reader—MCP		short a
The Big Cat	Ready Readers—MCP	5	short i
Jim Wins	Phonics Practice Reader—MCP		short i
Six Kids	Phonics Practice Reader—MCP		short i
Pop Pops the Popcorn	Ready Readers—MCP	7	short o
Hop On, Hop Off	Phonics Practice Reader—MCP		short o
Hot Rods	Phonics Practice Reader—MCP		short o
It's Hot	Ready Readers—MCP	5	short o, a
Dot	Bob Books—Scholastic		short o, a
What Is at the Top	Ready Readers—MCP	8	short o, i
Little Frog's Monster Story	Ready Readers—MCP	7	short o, i, a
Fix It Fox	Ready Readers—MCP	7	short o, i, a
The Lucky Duck	Ready Readers—MCP	7	short u
My Truck and My Pup	Teacher Created Materials		short u
Fun with Gum	Phonics Practice Reader—MCP		short u
Gus	Phonics Practice Reader—MCP		short u
Three Little Pigs and One Big Pig	Ready Readers—MCP	8	short u, i
Polly's Shop	Ready Readers—MCP	7	short u, o
Night and Day	Ready Readers—MCP	8	short u, i, a
Muff and Ruff	Bob Books—Scholastic		short u, i, a
The Best Places	Ready Readers—MCP	6	short e
Red Hen	Phonics Practice Reader—MCP		short e
Jet Bed	Phonics Practice Reader—MCP		short e
What Do We Have to Get?	Ready Reader—MCP	7	short e, a
I Can Swim	Ready Readers—MCP	6	short e, i
The Little Hen	Ready Readers—MCP	6	short e, o
Just Like Us	Ready Readers—MCP	7	short e, u
The Vet	Bob Books—Scholastic		short e, i, a
Lad and the Fat Cat	Bob Books—Scholastic		short e, o, i, a
The Trip	Ready Readers—MCP	7	short a, e, i, o, u
This Is Fred	Teacher Created Materials		short a, e, i, o, u

B.3. Leveled List of Books by Phonics Features—Books by Long vowels

Title of Book	Publisher	RR Level	Phonics Feature
The Name Is the Same	Ready Readers—MCP	11	a, e
That Cat!	Ready Readers—MCP	12	a, e
Save That Trash	Ready Readers—MCP	12	a, e
The Best Birthday Mole Ever Had	Ready Readers—MCP	8	a, e
Pancakes	Ready Readers—MCP	10	a, e
Kate and Jake	Phonics Practice Reader-MCP		a, e
Dave and His Raft	Phonics Practice Reader-MCP		a, e
Dive In!	Ready Readers—MCP	9	i, e
Dinner by Five	Ready Readers—MCP	9	i, e
The Bike That Spike Likes	Ready Readers—MCP	8	i, e
Jim's Visit to Kim	Ready Readers—MCP	12	i, e
Six Fine Fish	Ready Readers—MCP	10	i, e
The Princess and the Wise Woman	Ready Readers—MCP	18	i, e
Bike Hike	Phonics Practice Reader-MCP		i, e
The New Bike	School Zone	12	i, e
The Lion Roars	Ready Readers—MCP	15	i, e and a, e
I Like What I Am	Phonics Practice Reader-MCP		i, e and a, e
When Bob Woke up Late	Ready Readers—MCP	11	o, e
Sparky's Bone	Ready Readers—MCP	10	o, e
When I Go See Gram	Ready Readers—MCP	12	o, e
A Stew for Egor's Mom	Ready Readers—MCP	12	o, e

B.4. Publishers of Book Series for Emergent and Beginning Readers

Note: Most of these publishers sell series books (for example, *Sunshine Books* or *Twig* books are both series published by the Wright Group Company) rather than books by known authors. These series are marketed for use in schools and are generally not found in bookstores or libraries. When you call these publishers for catalogs or information, ask them if they can supply you with lists of books by Reading Recovery® levels since the publishers themselves may use various leveling systems.

Children's Press
   5440 North Cumberland Avenue
   Chicago, IL 60656-1469
   800-693-0800
   Series: *Rookie Readers*

Dominie Press, Inc.
   1949 Kellogg Avenue
   Carlsbad, CA 92008
   800-232-4570
   Fax 619-431-8777
   Series: *Carousel Readers and* others

Modern Curriculum Press
   4350 Equity Drive
   P. O. Box 2649
   Columbus, OH 43216
   800-321-3106
   Fax 614-771-7361
   Series: *Ready Readers* and *Phonics Practice Reader* (good for phonics connections)

Rigby
   P.O. Box 797
   Crystal Lake, IL 60039-0797
   800-822-8661
   Series: *Literacy 2000, Literacy Tree, PM Readers*, and others

Scholastic Inc.
   555 Broadway,
   New York, NY 10012
   800-325-6149
   Series: *Bob Books, Hello Readers, Phonics Readers*
   Also many paperback books by known authors

Sundance
   800-456-8204
   Fax 800-456-2419
   Series: *Little Red Readers*

Teacher Created Materials
   P.O. Box 1040
   Huntington Beach, CA 92647
   Series: *Easy Phonics Readers*

Wright Group
   19201 120th Avenue NE
   Bothell, WA 98011
   800-648-2970
   800-543-7323
   Series: *Story Box, Sunshine Readers, Twig,* and others

B.5 Order Form for Pictures to Use in Word Study for Phonics Sorts

---

Pictures for Sound Sorting Activities

This set of blackline masters contains an extensive collection of pictures for use in sorting beginning sounds and long and short vowel sounds. These pictures can be copied on card stock or paper to make multiple sets of pictures for use in classrooms or tutoring programs. The cost of the set is $12.00 plus $3.00 shipping & handling. Please include a check or purchase order with your order. If your tutoring program involves more than one school or 30 children, you should buy additional sets or contact me about copyright permission.

Francine R. Johnston

CUI Dept., School of Education

University of NC at Greensboro

Greensboro, NC 27412

Your Name _____

Address _____

_____

_____

B.6. Information on quantity discounts for *Book Buddies*

Quantity Discounts Available for *Book Buddies*

For multiple copies of *Book Buddies,* see the discount schedule below. Simply multiply the discount price per book by the quantity you are ordering. (Shipping is an additional 5% of your order.)

Quantity	List Price	Discount	Price Per Book
1 book	$19.95	—	$19.95
2–9 books		10% off list price	$17.95
10 copies or more		15% off list price	$16.95

Booksellers: Contact Guilford Customer Service for information about your applicable discount schedule for guided self-help titles, workbooks, and training manuals. Call toll-free 800-365-7006.

Training Videotapes for Volunteer Program Coordinators and Tutors

Vividly portraying the *Book Buddies* model in practice, two training videos for volunteers demonstrate tutorial sessions with emergent readers at different stages in the learning process. Each program reviews the Emergent Reader Lesson Plan outlined in the *Book Buddies* manual, with live footage of every component bringing the material to life. Presenters Marcia Invernizzi and Connie Juel provide extensive commentary on each session, explaining the rationale behind specific activities, discussing how to engage children and when and how to correct their mistakes, and offering pointers on methods and materials.

Emergent Reader—Day One
A Demonstration of Book Buddies in Action

Marcia Invernizzi and Connie Juel

It is the first week of school, and first-grader Ashley is eased into reading by her tutor, Marcia Invernizzi. Marcia helps Ashley feel like a successful reader despite her lack of knowledge of the alphabet and limited understanding of word boundaries. A home-made book, cards with the names of family members, a range of enjoyable reading activities, and lots of positive reinforcement begin to build Ashley's word bank and phonics knowledge and elicit her interest in the tasks at hand. Commentary from Marcia and copresenter Connie Juel illuminates each stage of the lesson plan: rereading familiar material, word study, writing for sounds, and introducing new reading materials.

51-Minute Color VHS, ISBN 1-57230-362-X, Cat. #0362, $29.95

Emergent Reader—Mid-Year
A Demonstration of Book Buddies in Action

Marcia Invernizzi and Connie Juel

This video features the mid-year work of tutoring volunteer Linda and her tutee, Tanisha, who have been meeting regularly since the beginning of school. Tanisha has gained limited fluency in reading, with knowledge of letters and beginning letter sounds. Proceeding through the four stages of rereading familiar material, word study, writing for sounds, and introducing new reading materials, Linda and Tanisha work on expanding Tanisha's word bank, creating a personal dictionary, mastering consonant blends and digraphs, and other goals. Throughout, explanatory remarks from presenters Marcia Invernizzi and Connie Juel review the specific skills being developed and the techniques Linda utilizes to do so.

44-Minute Color VHS, ISBN 1-57230-363-8, Cat. #0363, $29.95

For more information or to order any of these resources, contact Guilford Publications toll-free at 800-365-7006 or visit our Web site http://www.guilford.com.

Glossary

Blend. A blend is two or three consonants that are blended together to make a sound that retains the identities of each letter. For example, the word "stop" begins with an ST blend. When you say "stop," you hear both the "s" and the "t" sounds blended together. Blends occur at the beginning of words, as in "stop," and also at the end of words, as in "fast." In teaching children how to read, we focus mainly on the beginning blends. Other beginning blends include the BL in "blend," the BR in "brown," and the STR in "string."

Choral Reading. When two or more people read the same text at the same time, it is called choral reading.

Concept of Word. The ability to match spoken words to printed words in a one-to-one correspondence. This is demonstrated when children can accurately point with their finger as they read memorized text. If they get "off-track" and point to part of another word when they are saying something else, they don't have a concept of word. Children frequently get off-track on two-syllable words.

Consonants. The consonant letters are all the letters that are not vowels (see below). Consonants can usually be "felt" as we interrupt the flow of air through our vocal cords and mouth with our lips, tongue, teeth, and palate. Each of these words begins and ends with a consonant: "bed," "map," "fig," "lot."

Digraph. A digraph is a pair of letters that creates a single and unique sound. The new sound does not retain the identities of the individual letters. In this book, when we use the term "digraph," we are referring to the most common consonant digraphs that occur at the beginning of words: SH ("ship"), TH ("the" and "thin"), WH ("when"), and CH ("chip"). Consonant digraphs also occur at the end of words (as in "dish" and "each"), but in teaching children how to read, we focus mostly upon the beginning digraphs.

Early Reader. Early readers are able to do some reading on their own and know a number of words. They should be able to read at the primer level (which is equivalent to the middle of first grade) or above (up to early second-grade level)

Echo Reading. When readers reread or "echo" what has just been read to them.

Emergent Reader. Emergent readers may not be able to read anything at all, or they may be able to read only with a great deal of help in the earliest stages of first-grade materials (preprimer levels).

First-Grade Reading Level. In the traditional leveling system used by published basal readers, the first-grade level corresponds to the last third of first grade. In many basal series, this would be the 1.2 reader (first grade, second semester). Reading Recovery® levels 13–16 roughly correspond to the first-grade level.

High-Frequency Words. There are a small number of words that occur over and over in English. These most common words include "the," "of," "is," "were," and so on. In the past, these words were listed as Dolch Words. High-frequency words provide the "glue" for putting other words together in a meaningful sentence and have little meaning by themselves. They are often phonetically irregular (for example, "was"), and for this reason, beginning readers may have difficulty decoding and spelling those words.

Long Vowels. There are five common long vowel sounds. Long vowels "say their names"; that is, their sounds correspond to the name of their letter, as in "cake," "feet," "pride," "road," and "cute."

Patterns in Words. Certain combinations of letters work as a unit to represent sounds in words. We can see the AT pattern in these words: "cat," "mat," "sat." There are also spelling patterns that contain silent letters, which serve to "mark" the particular vowel sound of that letter. The silent "e" at the end of "cake," " home," and "tribe" has no sound of its own but in conjunction with the vowel in the middle forms a pattern: vowel, consonant, E (VCE). This pattern signals a long vowel sound in each word. English has many such patterns, especially for the long vowels.

Phonics. Phonics refers to the systematic correspondence between letters and sounds. Phonics is not a method of teaching reading, but refers to the knowledge of these letter–sound correspondences. There are many ways to teach children phonic generalizations.

Picture Sort. A picture sort is one phonics method. Pictures can be sorted into categories on the basis of particular sounds. In this book, there are activities for sorting pictures by beginning sounds, rhyming sounds or word families, and by the vowel sound in the middle.

Preprimer. In the traditional leveling system used by published basal readers, the preprimer level corresponded to the first one-third of the first-grade year. There were usually three paperback preprimers (PP1, PP2, PP3). Reading Recovery® levels 3–4 correspond roughly to PP1, levels 5–6 to PP2, and levels 7–8 to PP3.

Primer. In the traditional leveling system used by published basal readers, the primer level corresponded to the middle of first grade. The primer (pronounced with a short "i") was usually the first hardcover book and was sometimes referred to as the 1.1 reader (first grade, first semester). Levels 9–12 in the Reading Recovery® leveling system correspond roughly to the primer level.

Push It Say It. This is an activity developed by Blachman, Ball, Black, & Tangle (1994), to help children learn to blend sound chunks together to say words. "Push It Say It" involves the use of small cards that children push forward as they say the sound represented by the letter or letters on the card.

Readiness. This is a term used to refer to the stage of reading that precedes the preprimer level or the earliest stage of reading. Traditionally, children at the readiness stage were taught letter names and concepts of print, but were not expected to read.

Rhyming Chunk. This is a group of letters or a pattern that functions as a unit. Rhyming chunks occurs in word families that are spelled alike and rhyme. For example, the rhyming chunk AN occurs in these words: "can," "man," "fan," "pan," "than," "plan."

Timed Repeated Readings (TRR). This technique involves the child in reading and rereading the same passage of text three to five times. Each reading is timed, and errors are tallied. Progress can be charted on a graph.

Short Vowels. Each vowel has two major sounds: a long vowel and a short vowel. Short vowels are not "short" sounds. Short vowels are represented by the letters "a," "e," "i," "o," and "u," but the vowel sound associated with each does not mimic the name of the letter, as do the "long" vowels (which aren't any longer). Each of the short sounds is represented by the beginning letter in these words: "ax," "Eskimo," "igloo," "octopus," and "umbrella."

Vowels. Vowels are speech sounds that created by an unobstructed flow of air through the vocal cords and mouth. The vowel sounds are represented by the letters "a," "e," "i," "o," "u," and sometimes "y" (as in "my" and "myth"). The other letters of the alphabet represent consonant sounds.

Word Bank. This is a collection of words the child recognizes in isolation. Word bank-words are written on cards or small slips of paper and form a corpus for review and phonics study.

Word Families. All the words in a "family" rhyme and are spelled with the same pattern of letters. The ED family would include "bed," "red," "led," and "sled," but not "head."

Word Hunt. This is an activity in which children look through texts they have already read to find words that have particular sounds or spelling patterns.

Word Sort. A word sorts is a phonics method. In a word sort, word cards are categorized by a particular sound or by a particular spelling pattern that goes with that sound. In this book, there are activities for sorting words by beginning sounds, rhyming sounds or word families, and by the vowel sound in the middle. In addition, words may be sorted by spelling patterns such as the silent "e" pattern in "snake," "plate," and "tape" versus the AI pattern in "tail," "train," and "wait."

Index